"I've tried most every version of Holy Scripture. The *King James*, the *Revised Standard*, the *Living Bible*, the *Good News Bible*, and the *New International Version*. But not until I started using *Not the Bible* regularly, did I notice a direct co-relation between scriptural studies and sales. Thanks to *Not the Bible*, I sold more aluminum siding this year than anyone in the Tri-State region. I'd recommend it to anyone—except my competition!"

Joe Bob McJorrity
Sales Exec.—Mallville, Fla.

"Once I was vice-president of an advertising agency, earning three times as much as my husband. I had kids in Day Care and vacationed in the Islands, and I lobbied for the E.R.A. Now, since reading *Not The Bible*, I'm back in the kitchen, where I belong, and don't have a thought in my pretty little head."

Dolly (Mrs. Aaron) McJorrity
Housewife—Lawntown, Ga.

"When this world comes to an end in the inevitable nuclear exchange with the Russians, so clearly foretold in the Book of Revelations, I only hope and pray that every man, woman and child has a copy of *Not The Bible* in his fox hole!"

Gen. Curtis McJorrity
USMC (Ret'd.)—Condo, Ariz.

"The best way to drive out the devil, if he will not yield to texts of Scripture, is to jeer and flout him, for he cannot bear scorn."

M. Luther
Chaplain—Federal Republic of Germany

This

NOT

THE **B**IBLE

☐ *presented to*
☐ *inherited by*
☐ *sold to*
☐ *forced upon*
☐ *removed from a hotel room by*

_____

(YOUR NAME HERE)

**From the collection of
Lee Roger Taylor, Jr.
1944 - 1999**

Let us give thanks unto:
Art director David Kaestle, and
Associate Art director Leslie Engel.

And likewise unto:
Frederic Lewis, Inc., for blurb photos;
Richard Erlanger, for the Begat Tree illustration;
Jim Sherman, for the Book of News cartoon
and Book of Sodom cover;
the Bettman Archive
for the Book of News front page photo;
Frank Springer, for the David and Goliath comic art;
Cathy Canzani, for the Book of Visions art;
John O'Leary, for The Early Years cover;
Mari Kaestle, for the Magic Book illustrations;
David and Leslie, for the Love's Thorny Crown cover,
and Leslie herself, for Paul's map.

The Reverend Oral
was portrayed by "Thaddeus";
photographed by David Kaestle, and
styled by Veronica Reilly.

The authors are beholden
as well unto Christopher Cerf,
by whom this book was begotten, not made.

NOT
THE BIBLE

Containing

The Good Ol' Testament

and

The Neo-Testament

Translated Out of the Original English,
Condensed, Edited, Improved Upon and Authorized
by

The Reverend Oral McJorrity, D.D.

with the assistance of

Dr. Anthony Hendra and

Professor Sean Kelly

of the

Not The Bible Institute

Oral State University©

U.S.A.

Ballantine Books · New York

Library of Congress Catalog Card Number: 82-90826
ISBN: 0-345-30249-4

Manufactured in the United States of America

First Edition: February 1983

10 9 8 7 6 5 4 3 2 1

THE GOOD OL' TESTAMENT

The Book of Creation

The Begat Tree

The Book of Sodom

The Book of Onan

The Book of Rules

The Book of Comics

The Book of News

The Secret Life of Job

The Book of Products

The Book of Psongs

The Book of Proverbial Wisdom

The Book of More Products

The Book of Visions

The Oral Examination

THE NEO-TESTAMENT

Christ—The Early Years

Jesus H. Christ's
   Magical Traveling
   Medicine Show

The Wit and Wisdom of
   Jesus Christ

The Lord's School Prayer

Love's Thorny Crown

Epistles to the Apostle

Amazing Revelations

"Thank you very much. God bless you, thank you, and welcome to our Book!"

*L*adies and gentlemen, brothers and sisters, we have a truly Great Book for you here today. It's got fabulous characters with wonderful stories to tell, and it's chock-full of action, adventure, excitement, and good old-fashioned entertainment! We've got tales of love and hate, of sinners and saints, heaven and hell, good and evil, of absolutely fantastic miracles, and the every day trials and tribulations of every day people like you and I.

"It's a Book we like to call...Holy Scripture!

"Oh, I know what you're thinking now. You're thinking, 'Not the Bible!' And you're absolutely right! This is NOT THE BIBLE!

"Now the Bible's a Good Book. Make no mistake about it. It's the word of God, and we have God's own word for that fact. But, you take your average Bible. That one you have there in your bed-side night table drawer, next to the .38 automatic, for example.

"It's big. It's black. It's heavy. It's a whole lot of hard reading, isn't it? And, let's be honest, it's about as inspiring as an old umbrella.

"And, it's corrupt! Now, hold on a minute. What I mean by that is this: over the many centuries, false prophets and foreign translators, sloppy scribes, and, for all we know, secular humanists have been tampering with the Sacred Text!

"Let's turn, for an instance, to Matthew, Chapter 7, Verse 1. 'Judge not, that ye be not judged'. Now, what kind of advice is that for us Christians, trying to run a decent, law-abiding soci-

ety? Why the streets of our cities would be running with rampaging criminals, set loose by bleeding-heart courts!

"Not that they aren't...

"Now, I don't believe for one minute that the Savior ever said a thing like that, do you? Certainly not the personal Savior I get down on my knees and pray to every morning and every night, beside my virtuous and faithful wife, and our two handsome young sons, Oral Junior and Oral the Third!

"Or, turn, if you will, to the very first book of that so-called Bible you've got there. Genesis, it's called. Genesis! What kind of a name is that, with its connotations of sexual permissiveness?

"Furthermore, scan that text of 'Genesis' a moment, if you will. Sure, somewhere in that little-bitty hard-to-read type, it tells how God made the world, and made woman to serve man, and that the woman sinned...and all of that's true, and the word of God...as far as it goes.

"But what's essential *to our faith and our way of life sort of gets lost in there among all the flora and fauna and prose and poetry, doesn't it?*

"Because what's essential *is that you and I know and believe that* never, at no time, in no place, is there the slightest glimmer of a shadow of a possibility that there was ever such a process as so-called* Evolution!

"Am I right? You're damn right I'm right!

"So. Won't you all join with us now, as we turn the page together, and begin to read and to study the very lovely verses and the very simple chapters of..."

THE BOOK OF CREATION

CHAPTER 1

IN the beginning God created Dates.

2 And the date *was* Monday, July 4, 4004 B.C.

3 And God said, Let there be light; and there was light. And *when* there was Light, God saw the Date, *that* it was Monday, and he *got* down to work; for verily, he had a Big Job *to do*.

4 And God made pottery shards and Silurian mollusks and pre-Cambrian limestone strata; and flints and Jurassic Mastodon tusks and Picanthropus erectus skulls and Cretaceous placentals made he; and those cave paintings at Lasceaux. And that was *that*, for the first Work Day.

5 And God saw that he had made many wondrous things, *but* that he had not wherein to put *it* all. And God said, Let the heavens be divided from the earth; and *let* us bury all of these Things which we have made in the earth; *but* not too deep.

6 And God buried all the Things which he had made, and that was *that*.

7 And the morning and the evening *and* the overtime were Tuesday.

8 And God said, Let there be water; and let the dry *land* appear; and that was *that*.

9 And God called the dry *land* Real Estate; and the water called he *the* Sea. And in the land and beneath *it* put he crude *oil*, grades one through six; and *natural* gas put he thereunder, and prehistoric carboniferous forests yielding anthracite and other ligneous matter; and all these called he Resources; and *he* made them Abundant.

10 And likewise all that was *in* the Sea, even unto two hundred miles from the dry *land*, called he resources; all that was therein, *like* manganese nodules, for instance.

11 And the morning unto the evening *had been* an long day; *which* he called Wednesday.

12 And God said, Let the earth bring forth abundantly every moving creature I *can* think of, with or without back bones, with or without wings or feet, or fins or claws, vestigial limbs and all, right *now*; and let each *one* be of a separate species. For lo, I can make *whatsoever* I like, *whensoever* I like.

13 And the earth brought forth abundantly *all* creatures, great and small, with and without backbones, with and without wings and feet and fins and claws, vestigial limbs and all, *from* bugs *to* brontosauruses.

14 But God blessed them all, saying, Be fruitful and multiply and *Evolve Not*.

15 And God looked upon the species he had made, and saw that the earth was exceeding crowded, and he said *unto* them, Let each species compete for what it needeth; for Healthy Competition is My Law. And the species competeth amongst themselves, the cattle and the creeping things, the dogs and the dinosaurs; and some madeth it and some didn't; and the dogs ate the dinosaurs and God was pleased.

16 And God took the bones from the dinosaurs, and caused them to appear *mighty* old; and cast he them about the land and the sea. And he took every tiny *creature* that had not madeth it, and caused *them* to become fossils; and cast he them about *likewise*.

17 And just to put matters beyond the valley of the shadow of a *doubt* God created carbon dating. And *this* is the origin of

species.

18 And in the Evening of the day which *was* Thursday, God saw that he had put in *another* good day's work.

19 And God said, Let us make man in our image, after our likeness, *which is* tall and well-formed and pale of hue: and let us *also* make monkeys, which resembleth us not in any wise, *but* are short and ill-formed and hairy. And God added, Let man *have* dominion over the monkeys and the fowl of the air and every species, endangered or otherwise.

20 So God created Man in His *own* image; tall and well-formed and pale of hue created He him, and nothing at all like the monkeys.

21 And God said, Behold I have given you every herb bearing seed, which is upon the face of the earth. But ye shalt not smoketh it, *lest* it giveth *you* ideas.

22 And to every beast of the earth and every fowl of the air I have given also every green herb, and to them it shall be for *meat*. But they shall be *for you*. And the Lord God your Host suggesteth that the flesh of cattle goeth well with that of the fin and the claw; thus shall Surf be wedded unto Turf.

23 And God saw everything he had made, and he saw that it was very good; and God said, It *just* goes to show Me what the private sector can accomplish. With a lot of fool regulations this could have taken *billions of years*.

24 And on the evening of the fifth day, *which had been* the roughest day yet, God said, Thank me its Friday. And God made the weekend.

CHAPTER 2

T HUS the heavens and the earth were finished, and *all* in five days, and all less than six thousand of years *ago*; and if thou believest it not, in a sling *shalt* thou find thy hindermost quarters.

2 Likewise God took the dust of the ground, and the slime of the Sea and the scum of the earth and formed Man therefrom; and *breathed* the breath of life right in his face. And he *became* Free to Choose.

3 And God made an Marketplace eastward of Eden, in which the man was free *to* play. And this *was* the Free Play of the Marketplace.

4 And out of the ground made the Lord God *to grow* four trees: the Tree of Life, and the Liberty Tree, and the Pursuit of Happiness Tree, and the Tree of the Knowledge of Sex.

5 And the Lord God commanded the man, saying, This *is* my Law, which is called the Law of Supply and Demand. Investeth thou in the trees of Life, Liberty, and the Pursuit of Happiness, and thou shalt make for thyself an *fortune*. For *what* fruit thou eatest not, that thou mayest sell, and with the seeds thereof expand *thy* operations.

6 But of the fruit of the tree of the Knowledge of Sex, thou mayest not eat; nor mayest thou invest therein, nor profit thereby nor expand *its* operations; for that is a mighty waste of seed.

7 And the man was exceeding glad. But he asked the Lord God: Who then *shall* labor in this Marketplace? For am I not management, *being* tall and well-formed and pale of hue?

8 And the Lord God said unto himself, Verily, this kid hath the potential which is Executive.

9 And out of the ground the Lord God formed every beast of the field and every fowl of the air, and brought them unto Adam to labor for him. And they labored for peanuts.

10 Then Adam was again ex-

ceeding glad. But he spake once more unto the LORD God, saying, Lo, I am free to play in the Marketplace of the LORD, and have cheap labor in plenty; but to whom shall I sell my surplus fruit and realize a fortune thereby?

11 And the LORD God said unto himself, Verily, this is an Live One.

12 And he caused a deep sleep to fall upon Adam and he took from him one of his ribs, which was an spare rib.

13 And the spare rib which the LORD God had taken from the man, made he woman. And he brought her unto the man, saying:

14 This is Woman and she shall purchase your fruit, to eat it; and ye shall realize a fortune thereby. For Man produceth and Woman consumeth, wherefore she shall be called the Consumer.

15 And they were both decently clad, the Man and the Woman, from the neck even unto the ankles, so they were not ashamed.

CHAPTER 3

NOW the snake in the grass was *more* permissive than any beast of the field which the LORD God *had* made. And he said *unto* the woman, Why hast thou accepted this lowly and submissive *role*? For art thou not human, *even* as the man is human?

2 And the woman said unto the snake in the grass, The LORD God hath ordained that I am placed under the man, and must do whatsoever he telleth me to do; for is *he* not the Man?

3 But the snake in the grass laughed an cunning laugh, and said unto the woman, Is it not right and just that thou shouldst fulfill thy *potential*? For art thou not comely in thy flesh, even as the man is comely in his flesh?

4 And the woman said, Nay, I know not, for hath not the LORD God clad us decently, from the neck even unto the ankles; and forbidden that we eat of the Tree of the Knowledge of Sex?

5 But the snake in the grass said unto the woman, whispering even into her very ear, saying, Whatsoever feeleth good, do thou *it*; and believeth thou me, it feeleth *good*.

6 And when the woman saw the fruit of the Tree of the Knowledge of Sex, that it was firm and plump and juicy, she plucked thereof, and sank her teeth *therein*, and gave also to her husband, *and* he likewise sank his teeth *therein*.

7 And the eyes of *both* of them were opened, and they saw that they were not naked.

8 And the woman loosened *then* Adam's uppermost garment, and he likewise loosened hers; and she loosened his nethermost garment, and the man *then* loosened her nethermost garment; until they were out of their garments both, and *likewise* of their minds.

9 And, lo!, they did dance *upon* the grass of the ground, and they did rock backward, and roll forward continually;

10 And as they did rock and roll, the serpent that *was* cunning did play upon a stringéd *instrument* of music, and did smite his tail upon the ground in an hypnotic rhythm; and he did sing *in a voice* that was like unto four voices: She loveth you, yea, yea, yea.

11 And they did both twist and shout, and fall into an frenzy, both the man *and* the woman, and lay *themselves* upon the ground, and commit there abominations.

12 And when they *were* spent from their abominations, they did take the herb bearing seed, and did *roll* it and smoke it; and lo! it gaveth them ideas, even as the LORD God *had* said; and they were like *to commit* new abominations.

13 Now the LORD God was walking in the garden in the cool of the day, with his dog; and as

Adam and his wife were *beginning* these new abominations, the LORD God did stub the toe of his *foot* upon their hindermost quarters.

14 And the LORD God *waxed* wroth, and said unto Adam, Wherefore art thou naked? And what is *that* thou smokest? And why art thou not at thy *work*? For have I not said that it is the man's part to produce, and the part of the woman to consume whatsoever he produceth?

15 And Adam and his wife did look *upon* one another, and did giggle.

16 Whereupon the LORD God waxed exceeding wroth, and he said, Hast thou eaten of the tree, whereof I commanded *thee* that thou *shouldst* not eat?

17 And the man said, The woman *whom* thou gavest to be *with me* made me do it.

18 And the LORD God said unto the woman, What is *this* that thou hast done? And the woman said, The snake in the grass made me do it.

19 And the snake in the grass said, The devil made *me* do it.

20 And the LORD God said unto the snake in the grass, Thou art an permissive *beast*; wherefore art thou cursed to crawl upon thy belly, and be *made into* belts and boots and handbags hereafter.

21 Unto the woman He said, Since thou hast harkened unto the snake in the grass which is broad-of-mind and permissive; henceforth let it be thy lot to be confused and *scattered* in thy brains, and to be plagued by demons who shall tempt thee to become that which thou canst not be: such as an warrior, or an extinguisher of fires, or an operator of heavy machinery.

22 And since thou hast put aside the decent clothing wherein I clad thee, here after no garment *shall* satisfy thee, and thou shalt be overcome by longings to change thy raiment *every* spring and fall.

23 And above all this, since thou hast desired to taste of the fruit of the Tree of the Knowledge of Sex, now let thy *very* body be a curse unto thee. From generation unto generation, men *shalt* whistle and hoot after thee *as* thou passest; yea, and women also.

24 And unto Adam he said, Woe unto thee who hast harkened not to the voice of the LORD thy God, but rather to her who is *thy* inferior; for thou wast free to choose. Now shalt thou be banished from the Marketplace and the Free Play thereof; *neither* shalt thou pluck the fruit from the Trees of Life and Liberty and the Pursuit of Happiness.

25 In the sweat of thy face *shalt* thou earn thy bread, and bankruptcy shall be *thy* lot; and upon thy back, as a burden *unto* thee, thou shalt bear Big Government; for thou hast sinned.

26 And the LORD God said unto the man, Behold, thy knowledge of sex shall be as a curse upon thee and thy generations; and thy loins shall be a trial unto thee.

27 For whensoever thou goest into a public place, *then* shall thy member rise *up*; when thou sitteth to eat and drink among thy fellows, likewise shall it rise *up*; yea, even when thou standeth before the people to preach unto *them* in *my* name, shall it rise *up*, and be a scandal unto thee, and make an unseemly lump *in* thy garments; yet when thou goest into thy wife shall thy member wither, and rise *up* not.

28 And then the LORD God was silent, and waxed sad, and made as if to leave them *there*. But he turned, and spoke softly *unto* Adam and his wife Eve, saying, Knowest thou *something*? Mine *only* hope is this: That someday, ye have children who do *unto* you the way ye have done *unto* Me.

"There now.
Wasn't that better?"

No hard-to-understand words or other corruptions and confusions. Just a plain, age-old story. God makes the world, and He's happy. God makes Man, and they're both happy. God makes woman. She's unhappy—and pretty soon, everybody's unhappy!

"A simple chain of events—and not a 'missing link' in it anywhere!

"Now, of course, that's not all that happens in the Book of so-called Genesis.

"There's the story of how Abel, a nice enough fellow in his way, forgets that sometimes a Man's got to stand up and kill for what's right, and Cain makes him pay the price. There's a lesson there for us all.

"Then everything goes along pretty well for about fifteen hundred years, until the women commence fornicating with giants, and the Lord, who you will remember describes himself elsewhere as a jealous God, sends the great Flood, to teach them a thing or two.

"Not a single human being survived that Flood, except for Noah, and his sons, and their wives—and, of course, Methuselah, who the Bible says was only 870 years old when it hit, but lived to 969 years of age. Say "Amen."

"But a great many pages of Genesis, not to mention Numbers and Chronicles, are taken up by long lists of who begat who, back then.

"So, to make things easier for the busy modern Christian, a crack team of Not The Bible scholars and researchers here at Oral State University© has compiled and condensed this genealogy, into what we like to call The Begat Tree.

"Let's give it a real nice round of applause."

NORMAN
LEAR
β
CLARENCE
DARROW
β
HITLER FREUD
β ANDY YOUNG
MARX β CHARLES β β
DARWIN MUHAMMAD ALI
β β
STALIN BENEDICT ARNOLD CHUCK BERR
β β β
GEORGE III NAT TURN
E. β β
ROOSEVELT DRACULA HO CHI MINH HO
β β β
JANE ATTILA THE HUN MAO TSE TUNG
FONDA β
JUDAS ISCARIOT FU MANCHU
β β
KING HEROD BUDDAH
β β
MUSICIANS, ARTISTS AND
"ALL WHO LIVE IN TENTS"
(I.E. ARABS AND ECO-NUTS)
β β
PHARAOH ENOCH
β β
NEBUCHADNEZZAR
β CAIN–
MOHAMMED GIANT'S DAUGHTER
β (ANON)
AYATOLLAH KHOMEINI β
β CAIN ABI
YASIR ARAFAT β β

ADAN
= EV.
β
GOD =
ADAN

Nubian

Branch

Evil

The

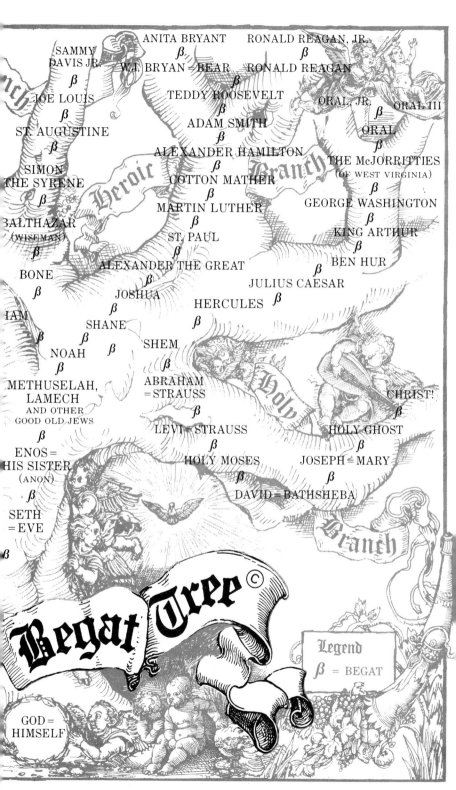

I *t's not easy, being a Patriarch today. There are so many demands, expectations, duties, worries, and expenses. But the Scriptures, in their eternal, prophetic wisdom, hold the answer to each and every problem we might face, and Divinely Inspired Examples for us to follow! Let us consider the works and deeds of those Saints of old . . . And let us pray."*

Prayer for the Patriarch with Teenage Sons (Gen. 28)

Lord, Thou Who seest and understandest all, go figure kids today. Dost Thou, who didst command Thy servant Abraham to slay his son, knowest what I mean? Give me strength, O Lord, this day to do like unto Thy servant Isaac did unto his son Esau, and cast him out from my sight; for is my son not likewise hairy? Amen.

Prayer for the Patriarch with Teenage Daughters (Gen. 19)

O Lord, Who didst in Thy infinite mercy contrive to save Thy servant Lot not from destruction only, but also from his wife; grant that like unto Lot I may drink wine until I am drunken, and be no longer responsible for my actions, and that my teenage daughters may come in unto me, and it won't be my fault, and lie with me, one at a time, without my having hardly any idea what's happening, or better still, lie with me both together, O Lord! Amen.

Prayer for the Patriarch of a Business Concern (Gen. 27-35)

Lord, Thou knowest what it's like to run a Big Operation. Grant that I may study the words of Thy Holy Writ, and follow the example of Thy servant Jacob, who didst by craft and guile cut his brother out of the action, and thereafter take from Laban his herds and daughters and treasure, by stealth and cunning. Suffer my competition to come unto me to be circumcised, that I may strike a deal with them, and the next day slay them while they are sore and can't walk, even; that my seed may be fruitful and my dividends multiply, forever and ever. Amen.

Men of Sodom!

ABRAHAM AND LOT
ARE LOOKING FOR
TEN RIGHTEOUS MEN

Are You Behind Us?

Art Thou a Sodomite?

Answer thou "Yea" or "Nay" unto the following
questions.

1. Dwelleth thou in:
            a) Zoar?
            b) Mamre?
            c) Sodom or Gomorrah?

2. When thou beholdest a goat, exclaimest thou:
            a) A fitting sacrifice unto the LORD!?
            b) Yum yum! Good eats!?
            c) Oh, you kid!?

3. Thongs of leather are purposed for:
            a) The just chastisement of thy wife
               and offspring?
            b) The harnessing of beasts?
            c) Wearing tightly wrapped about thy body?

4. When thous visiteth the bath, why doest thou so:
            a) For to cleanse thyself ritually?
            b) For to repair the plumbing thereof?
            c) For to lounge around in thy towel?

5. Whensoever thou hearest spoken the word "date,"
   thinkest thou immediately of:
            a) 4004, B.C.?
            b) Yum yum! Good eats!?
            c) Thy fellow man?

6. From the rising up of the sun to the setting
   thereof, art thou:
            a) Offering sacrifice unto the LORD,
               whilst thy wife decorateth thy tent?
            b) Tilling thy fields, whilst thy wife
               decorateth thy tent?
            c) Decorating thy tent?

7. The Rod of God; when thou considereth it, dost thou
   say in the fastness of thy heart:
            a) I exalt in the downfall of mine
               enemies?!?
            b) Woe unto me, in my sinfullness!?
            c) Yum yum! Good eats!?

1: If thou answereth "Yea" but one time unto any of the seven (c)s, then art thou damned out of thy own mouth, and thy loins shall be fruitless; yea, thou shalt be cast into a dark place, and degraded, and struck with strong blows, even when thou desireth it not; for surely thou art a Sodomite, and a Gomorrahite, to boot!

2: If thou answereth (b) even one time only, surely thou needeth work. For thou yet may backslide into Gluttony, and Drunkeness, and other abominations of the flesh. Place thyself firmly, therefore, in the hands of Abraham and Lot.

3: But if thou answereth (a) unto all questions, then surely thou art a righteous man, and upstanding. Thy path is clear, yea, and thy way is clean. For we say unto thee, holdest thou not thyself back, but come thou together with us, even unto the desert; put thou away thy wives and concubines, and join thou unto us, forever and ever, Amen.

Righteous Men of Sodom, hasten away! For Straight is the way of the Lord!

The LORD God in his wrath shall destroy and over-throw all that which is in the Cities of the Plain!

And He shall rain in brimstone and in fire upon all furnishings which are ancient, and upon them that dealeth in them!

And upon them that drinketh the drink which is mimosa, and eateth the eggs which are Benedict, and all that is brunch; shall He rain in fire!

And upon them that worship the Piggy and the Cat, which are unclean; and maketh books thereof, wherein the Piggy and the Cat are made to utter cute things;

Likewise shall He rain fire and brimstone upon all those that cut and braid the hair of women, and fawn much upon them, and privily call them Bitch! Therefore, make haste, O men of Sodom!

FOR THY END IS AT HAND!

*T*he word "seed" appears a lot in the Scriptures. We hear of the seed of Adam, the seed of Abraham, the seed of Isaac and Jacob. Just about every normal, healthy Biblical male had seed.

"Now seed here doesn't mean seed like you put in your lawn. It means something much dirtier, which should only be discussed in private, by qualified Christian adults. One thing we can say about seed, though, right out here on paper, is that it belongs in ONE PLACE and ONE PLACE ONLY.

"And that's IN YOUR WIFE.

"Luckily Abraham, Isaac, Jacob, and Company knew where to put their seed, or we'd be in plenty of trouble today! But there was one person back there who, even though he knew better, didn't put his seed in the right place. His name was ONAN and he's one of the few real sinners in the Good Book. Instead of putting his seed where it belonged, he SPILLED IT ON THE GROUND!

"Now, the so-called Old Testament only gives us one example of Onan's sin (seems he took a shine to his brother's wife and went ahead with some spilling), but there were many other examples of his disgusting behavior. Horrible and immoral though these were, we can learn from them. We can learn how not to get ourselves into situations where WE might be tempted to...SPILL OUR SEED UPON THE GROUND!

"To get this point over, I'm going to give you these other examples, and after each one, I want you to say all together with me: "....HE SPILLED HIS SEED UPON THE GROUND!"

"We'll start with that little episode of his brother's wife, so that you can get the idea. OK? Here we go with:"

THE BOOK OF ONAN

NOW there dwelt in the land of Canaan, the son of Judah, one Onan, and his brother was married to a wife named Tamar who was right comely; and one day Onan took an augur and drilled a hole in Tamar's door while that she was shedding her undergarments. And putting his eye to the hole, he gazed upon his sister-in-law's naked loins and...[*All together now!*]...

HE SPILLED HIS SEED UPON THE GROUND!

AND another time, Onan was just sitting around the house doing nothing, although there was plenty to do, and he came upon some of Tamar's undergarments, the which she had laundered; and he fell to fondling them and caressing them, and pretty soon...

HE SPILLED HIS SEED UPON THE GROUND!

YEA Onan was an idle man and there were many things in his father's house that gave him idle thoughts; as long fruits and vegetables, wineskins, and raw meat. These would he ponder and toy with and more often than not...

HE SPILLED HIS SEED UPON THE GROUND!

ONCE he even stuck his finger in a clam and felt around inside and...

HE SPILLED HIS SEED UPON THE GROUND!

NOW Onan was wont to go forth unto that part of the City where filthy tablets were permitted to be sold. These would he purchase and gaze upon. And some were of women which committed abominations with men...

AND HE SPILLED HIS SEED UPON THE GROUND!

AND others showed women that lay with women...

AND HE SPILLED HIS SEED UPON THE GROUND!

OR with dogs...

AND HE SPILLED HIS SEED UPON THE GROUND!

YET loved he best that tablet wherein another man spilled *his* seed upon the ground...

AND HE SPILLED HIS SEED UPON THE GROUND!

NOW in that same part of the City where it was permitted to sell filthy tablets, were presented all manner of lewd shows. And one day Onan bought a ticket to a show wherein two women did wrestle in a tub of mud...

AND HE SPILLED HIS SEED UPON THE GROUND!

AND then came one who mocked the God-fearing and advocated lewdness and used racy language...

AND HE SPILLED HIS SEED UPON THE GROUND!

AND finally a band of musicians which were but scantily clad and played loud music with a beat that was the beat of his heart so that the blood rushed to his privates...

AND HE SPILLED HIS SEED UPON THE GROUND!

AND after the show, did Onan go unto a party where he swore and cursed using explicit sexual terms which inflamed him so mightily that...

HE SPILLED HIS SEED UPON THE GROUND!

AND he drank of strong drink and put smokables in his face, and drew smoke into his lungs which stimulated his glands and again...

HE SPILLED HIS SEED UPON THE GROUND!

AND all the women in that place eschewed restraining under-garments so that their parts were visible especially their dugs, whereof the eager nipples strained against the tightness of their sweaters, and Onan...

SPILLED HIS SEED UPON THE GROUND!

AND as if that were not enough, he went home to bed and what did he do?

HE SPILLED HIS SEED UPON THE GROUND!

NOW soon the thought of any woman's body in its nakedness, whether of his mother or his sister or his cousin or his aunt, would cause Onan's member to rise up...

AND HE SPILLED HIS SEED UPON THE GROUND!

NAUGHT was sacred to Onan. Once whilst assisting at Divine Service Onan beheld a fair maiden in the front row; and though she was dressed modestly withal yet could he discern that her dugs were huge. And he fell to thinking on their roundness and softness and right there in church...

HE SPILLED HIS SEED UPON THE GROUND!

YEA, Onan became a desperate case! If he went walking in the woods and beheld a tree whereof the limbs were cleft and in the cleft was an knot-hole...

HE SPILLED HIS SEED UPON THE GROUND!

AND if he went walking in the fields and beheld an ewe; and the ewe was white and wooly and her hindermost portions were towards him...

HE SPILLED HIS SEED UPON THE GROUND!

AND if he went forth into the city and beheld a great pillar raised up to the glory of the Lord and the pillar was round and long and thick and smooth...

HE SPILLED HIS SEED UPON THE GROUND!

AND before long, any hole, or crack, or long thing or soft thing, yea any *thing* whatsoever would put him in mind of fornication...

AND HE SPILLED HIS SEED UPON THE GROUND!

AND first five, then ten, then a score of times each day would his hand seek his privateness...

AND HE SPILLED HIS SEED UPON THE GROUND!

AND then his wife, who verily was an unfortunate woman, for that he put not his seed where it belonged, came unto him, crying "Onan, Onan, get a hold of yourself!" And he did...

AND HE SPILLED HIS SEED UPON THE GROUND!

AND when the LORD saw that Onan heeded not the words of her wherein he should place his seed, the LORD determined to slay Onan, as an example to His people and to stop the terrible waste of seed. Yet Onan repented not; and even at the moment of his death, he grasped his manliness, and, crying out with a great voice, said "I'm coming God! Oh God, I'm coming!"

AND HE SPILLED HIS SEED UPON THE GROUND!

AMEN

HERE ENDETH THE BOOK OF ONAN

"This is Timmy. Timmy is as blind as a bat..."

His IQ has dropped from 131 to 58 in just six short months. Timmy has to shave his right palm at least three times a day to prevent beard-like growth from engulfing his hand.

"Why? Because Timmy is a chronic Onanist! Groping for that easy pleasure, that quick fix, that momentary "high," Timmy has reduced himself to a babbling vegetable, pumping out the precious fluid of his immortal soul by the bucketful.

"Timmy was not always like this. Till recently his God-fearing parents had protected him from such Un-Christian subjects as where babies come from and why his sister is different from him. But then his school—a publicly financed school, I'd like to add, financed by your taxes, just like I am—this school began a so-called SEX EDU-CATION PROGRAM!! Daily, Timmy was encouraged to draw the private parts of young girls on the blackboard and fondle "anatomically correct" models of NAKED men and women! Is it any wonder that before long little Timmy was SPILL-ING HIS SEED like a lawn-sprinkler?! There isn't much we can do for Timmy now. We can buy him a guide dog, trim his palm, padlock his pants. But apart from that, nothing. Timmy will die soon and go to hell. And all because some faceless bureaucrat thought he ought to know the difference between a v----a and a p---s!

"Folks, let's prevent other young Christians from slipping into the slimy pit of onanism. Let's get sex out of education, and back in the dark, where it belongs. The problem with sex is mounting all the time. But if we take it in hand we can beat it! One day, God willing, we'll even be able to lick it! But we need money folks. Lots of it. So send lots of money to me, Oral McJorrity c/o THE ORAL STATE CENTER FOR SELF ABUSE©.

"Thank you."

"The Lord loves Law'n'Order!"

*A*fter the fall of Sodom, Jacob's family and the other descendants of Abraham went to live in the land of Egypt, at the personal invitation of the Pharaoh. But (and perhaps there is a lesson here for all of us today), the Egyptians went back on their word, and tried to turn the Hebrews into slaves! That was when old Moses, acting on an Executive Order from God Himself, led the Exodus, right through the Red Sea!

"Then, in the wilderness, at Mount Sinai (yes, my friends, that very same Sinai that the descendants of Moses have been bamboozled into handing over to those same double-dealing Egyptians!) God made his Covenant with the Israelites.

"Now, just what is a Covenant? Well, in Hebrew, the word is "Berith," which means, literally, "a deed." So we could say that this Covenant between God and Moses (who had power of attorney for all Israel) was a deed—the result of a real estate deal—a lease, if you will—by which the Greatest LANDLORD of Them All, the LANDLORD God of Hosts, allowed the Israelites to occupy the Promised Land. Naturally, there were terms and conditions of payment and behavior.

"This deed, or Covenant, which was written on stone by the flaming finger of God Himself, is—with the exception of the Declaration of Independence—the most important document in the history of the world! And here it is now! Ladies and gentlemen..."

The Book of Rules

Covenant

made this *July 4* day of *1,100 B.C.*,

between *The Lord God Jehova, Yawveh, Elohim Adonai*

, party of the first part

hereinafter referred to as God,

and *The Hebrew Nation, Seed of Abraham, Twelve Tribes of Israel*

, parties of the second part,

hereinafter referred to as The Chosen People.

Witnesseth:

That God bestows upon the Chosen People,

and the Chosen People gratefully and humbly accept from God,

the premises known as *The Promised Land (extending from the Red Sea unto the Sea of the Philistines)*

for the term of

Eternity

(or until such term shall sooner cease and expire,

as hereinafter provided);

the present and/or future occupation of said premises by

Canaanites, Moabites, Edomites and other Arabs

Not withstanding.

Terms and Conditions: 1. I am the LORD thy God. Thou shalt not make unto thee any graven images, to bow down thyself before them; save and except they be of an Eagle, or a flag, or something similarly patriotic.

2. Thou shalt not take the name of the LORD thy God in vain; but he shall be held guiltless who taketh it to put it upon his currency, and likewise he who sweareth falsely by it in matters of National Security.

3. Remember the Sabbath day, to keep it wholly miserable for thyself and thy neighbors.

4. Honor thy father and thy mother; but Medicare is going too far.

5. Thou shalt not kill the innocent babe in the womb. After it's born— open season.

6. Thou shalt not commit adultery, women especially.

7. Thou shalt steal.

8. Thou shalt declare for business against big labor.

9. Thou shalt not call up thy neighbor's wife.

10. Thou shalt not covet thy neighbor's house; but thou shalt work thy buns off, or better yet cause others to work their buns off for thy sake, and thereby acquire such a house as thy neighbor shall covet of thee.

Additional Articles: LIKEWISE, the Chosen People warrant and pledge for the term of this Covenant, themselves, their heirs, seed, distributees, slaves, executors, concubines, administrators, kings, judges, successors, and assigns, as follows:

1. That they shall refrain from eating the flesh of such unclean creatures as camels, rabbits, pigs, shrimp, four-legged birds, vultures, and mice;

2. That they shall abstain from such unclean practices as homosexuality, bestiality, incest, and shaving the corners of their beards;

3. That, in the event of leprosy, menstruation, seminal emission, or the discharge (voluntary or involuntary) of phlegm, drool, earwax, toe-jam, dandruff, and all other bodily secretions, including, but not limited to, blood, sweat, and tears; the secreter of same, (hereinafter referred to as The Sinner) shall forthwith immerse him/herself and any object, animate or inanimate, which he/she has either touched or thought about touching, into a tub of boiling water, or at least a very hot shower, and say "I'm sorry."

Rent: IN return for sole and exclusive Divinely ordained occupation of the premises, the Chosen People shall render unto God, at such altar or temple as God may designate, such sacrifices as God may, from time to time, demand; including, but not limited to, burnt offerings in the form of first-born bullocks, suckling lambs, ram's rumps, and plucked turtle doves, and:

One half (½) shekel *per* Chosen man, woman and child, *per annum*, or fifteen percent (15%) of the annual gross income of each and every Chosen man, woman, and child, whichever is greater.

Agency Clause: SUCH due rental payments of both burnt offerings and shekels shall be rendered unto the authorized fiscal agents of God, *i.e.*, any minister, elder, presbyter, priest, rabbi, evangelist, parson, pastor, prelate, dean, deacon, or vicar; that is, any clergyman, self- or otherwise ordained.

Ram Jubilee:
HERE is a recipe for a burnt offering which Aaron and his sons have always found especially acceptable:

1. Thou shalt take one ram (without blemish);

2. Thou shalt slay the ram;

3. Thou shalt cut the ram in pieces, and wash the inwards of him with water;

4. Thou shalt remove from the ram the fat and the rump, the caul above the liver, the 2 kidneys and the fat that is upon them. Thou shalt remove also and set aside the right shoulder;

5. As with every oblation of thy meat offering, shalt thou season it with salt;

6. Thou shalt roast the ram slowly over a shittim wood fire, basting often thereon with a sauce, which is called Leviticus;

7. The Sauce Leviticus thou shalt make as follows: with equal parts of the principal spices, pure myrrh, sweet cinnamon, sweet calamus, and cassia, and frankincense; mingle a fourth part of an hin of beaten oil olive, and a tenth deal of fine wheaten flour;

8. Thou shalt serve this offering with green ears of corn dried by the fire as a dish of the side, together with an hin of wine for a drink offering.

In Witness Whereof,
God and the Chosen People have respectively signed and sealed this Covenant.

God
Moses

ILLUSTRATED

BIBLE STORIES

FOR LITTLE ONES

In this issue:
DAVID
and
GOLIATH

WEATHER OUTLOOK: Continuing Exile— Rain of Frogs Unlikely

THE BOOK OF NEWS

"BABYLON'S LARGEST SELLING NEWS *PAPYR*"

FIERY FURNACE CAPER

3 SUSPECTS GRILLED

STORY, PHOTO PAGE 2

Continued From Page 1

FIERY FURNACE CAPER:

3 SUSPECTS GRILLED

BABYLON, 585 B.C.: Palace Authorities today released the names of three alleged accomplices of the notorious Jewish lawyer, lion tamer and quack psychoanalyst, Daniel, now in custody.

The trio, identified as Hananiah (alias Shadrach), Mishael (a.k.a. Meshach) and Azariah (assumed name, Abednego) have been held for questioning, in a plot to overthrow the Nebuchadnezzarian regime.

Palace Security Forces have been granted permission to employ a wide variety of interrogation techniques on the suspected rebels, despite the usual objections on their behalf by their attorney, Daniel.

Claiming that the three are "children," Daniel maintained that the government had violated his clients' rights by placing them in the Fiery Furnace, but he was overruled by Judge Belteshazzar, who cited "society's need to protect itself' from these roving bands of over-privileged teenagers who have been taking the law into their own hands."

Upon hearing Daniel's sarcastic aside that he had "feet of clay," the judge slapped the controversial de-

EZEKIAL SIGHTS U.F.O.

A thirty-year-old Israeli immigrant allegedly experienced a "close encounter," a fearful sighting of what appeared to be nothing less than a glowing spacecraft, hovering over the river Chebar last night.

Ezekial, identified by fellow members of the Hebrew community as a clergyman and "the son of Buzi," was clearly in a state of shock after seeing the four enormous "dreadful wheels," and could only mumble and rant incoherently about the "astronauts" within, who, he says, had four wings and four faces each, "but straight feet."

RETRACTION

The scribes and pharisees of this Newspapyr would like to personally and officially apologize for the publication of an item in yesterday's "Jeremiads" column.

Although the author of "Jeremiads," Baruch, is allowed a certain amount of prophetic license, his accusations of *voyeurism* against two respected Elders were both irresponsible and false.

Our columnist's only "source" for the "Peeping Elder" story was the woman herself. Susanna, who is notorious throughout Babylon for her custom of bathing nude in her husband's garden.

We deeply regret any embarrassment or inconvenience caused to the two respected Elders, and unhesitatingly retract the story as utterly Apocryphal.

LAMENTORIAL

GOOD FIGS AND NAUGHTY FIGS

Blessed are they who believeth in a strong Judah, opineth thy prophet!

A strong Judah shall stand as a bastion of theocracy against the heathen Syrians and Persians and Egyptians!

But woe unto them whose mouths are loud, and whose heads are hot, and who would depart from this land of plenty.

Yelling that the Lord God hath bidden them to return unto Judah and dwell therein!

Left of wing are such as these, boat-rockers, makers-of-trouble, pointy-heads, panty-waists, head-in-the-clouders!

O Judah, thou needest not such as the extremist Daniel and the accursed assassin Ishmael, and their like; for they are full of dung, and their words are like a hot wind and naught hangeth between their thighs!

Neither do we in Babylon need them here, for they would tear down that which we have built up, and

Missives to the Scribes

...or, I say unto you, hath not Babylon been good to us? Are we not partners in its prosperity, sitting here by its waters, making money hand over fist? This is captivity? I say unto you: With enemies like this who needeth friends?

O Judah, thou needest not empty words and heads, but MONEY for adequate defenses!

Rock-hard walls in Jerusalem thou needest; and swords and shields and long-range spears, that thou might endure against the foes of freedom in this troubled spot!

Ever see such as Daniel or Ishmael shelling out a shekel for the defense of Judah, or to sow her with trees even?

Verily I say unto ye, ye shall see it not, for such as they have not worked a day in their lives!

Evil are they, and rotten, and like unto a basket of naughty figs!

Righteous men should put the sandal to their hindquarters, and put it there NOW!

(Thy prophet welcometh responsible replies)

Traffic Woes

Dear Sirs,
This city is an abomination! Chariots are raging in the streets, and jostling one another! A person can't hear himself think for the noise of the whip and the rattling of the wheels! Where are Rab-mag and the rest of the Guards when we need them?
NAHUM
Nineveh

Esther Shmesther!

Dear Sirs:
"Esther, Esther, Esther!" I'm sick of hearing about her! Doesn't anybody remember Jezebel? Now, she was a *real* Queen, until they let her career go to the dogs!
HABAKKUK
Chaldea

Sanitation Woes

Sirs,
May I join those bringing to your attention the deplorable condition of all the gates, and especially the dung gate?
NEHEMIAH
Jerusalem

Defense Woes

Sirs,
I thinketh I speaketh for all other firm Hebrew Nationals when I sayeth in a loud voice that we wax sick and tired of your prophets Isaiah and Micah wailing and whining about 'peace'!

Are the Babylonians beating their swords into ploughshares? Dost thou notice the Assyrians beating their spears into pruning hooks? Thou wagerest thy hindermost quarters otherwise! Waketh up!
JOEL
The Valley of Decision

The Nostalgia Column

Remembering Zion

100 Years Ago Today. (640, B.C.) No sooner was Manasseh in the cold cold ground than teen-age monarch Josiah initiated a vast Temple-Renewal project. Grafitti were erased, idols purged, and when Molech was kicked in the bolechs, that was the old Baal game!

200 Years Ago Today. (740, B.C.) From the Gulf of Aqaba in the south, all the way to Damascus, Jereboam II (The King-Sized) ruled the Promised Land. For once, the borders of Israel were secure!

500 Years Ago Today. 1040, B.C.) Ace handicapper Samuel the Wise picked Little David of Bethlehem to outrun Big Saul in the first annual Punch and Judah Sweepstakes.

1000 Years Ago Today. (1540, B.C.) Yaweh and Moses continued to engage in "frank and open" negotiations at the Summit Talks over Sinai. Both sides agreed to return to the tablets tomorrow.

5000 Years Ago Today. (5540, B.C.) Nothing. Earth without form; darkness on the face of the deep.

Book Bonus!

The Book of Esther

The Story of a Jewish Assyrian Princess

Synopsis: Babylon, in the time of Captivity. Raven-haired starlet Esther is so lovely, no one guesses she is Jewish. She has won a beauty pageant promoted by her uncle Mordecai, and married Xerxes, the black-bearded and tempestuous King of Persia. But now Xerxes has departed for ancient

"Thermopylae, Shmermopylae!" screamed the Princess, "What about *my* nails!"

JEREMIADS

Talkest thou about man biteth dog? What sayest thou to *fish* eateth *man*? It seemeth that *Jonah*, Nineveh's favorite stand-up prophet, hath them rolling in the aisles with a story about spending three days in the belly of a fish! Why didst he that? "Just for the halibut," sayeth the prophet. "Nay, but verily," he addeth, "I performed my act therein. And on the third day, it vomited me out upon the dry land! These days, everybody's a critic!"

Crowned Heads:

According to Asphenaz (a *prince* among eunuchs, by the way) *King Nebby* is at it again! Talkest thou about feet of clay? It seemeth that his Highness hath been dreaming of huge metal trees and monsters growing long his nails and hair, and that he eateth *grass!*

Soundeth to us like he *smoketh* grass! *Evil Merodach* (how likest thou *that* for a name?) still standeth to inherit the throne, but the money which is smart is upon Belshazzar.

Babble On, Babylon!

Invite not to the same feast: *Hosea* and his wife ... *Jehoiachin* made King of Judea in exile. Who cares? ... Amazing look-alikes: *Gog* and *Magog* ... What ever happened to *Maher-shalal-hash-baz*? Big food fight *clutches of Haman, the evil prime minister...*

Until tomorrow, remembereth thou the words of the prophet: I like not to say unto thee that I told thee so, *but*... I told thee so!

She was Queen of Bablyon. Wealth, money, riches—she had it all. But Esther lived in fear. Would the King guess her secret?

Crazy King Nebby

All night on her queen-sized bed of silken sheets, Esther tossed and turned. Sleep would not come. She listened as, in the throne room below, the courtiers had loudly rattled the dice of Purim till dawn, vowing death to every Jew! As the sun rose, the royal carpenters began hammering away beneath her window, constructing the gallows from which to hang her uncle!

Now, as she pulled up the silken coverlet, she felt one of her long, magnificent scarlet fingernails break. "Why does *everything* happen to me?" she could not help but think!

Suddenly, she heard shrill shrieks of surprise from the ante-chamber, where her maid-servants and eunuchs slept. It sounded as if a mighty python had appeared in a cage of doves, or an invading army of Spartans!

Her hang-nail for the moment forgotten, the Princess leapt out of bed, and she felt her heart beat faster.

Thrusting aside the plush draperies of her portal, King Xerxes himself boldly strode into her chamber. He was still wearing his armor, his black eyes were smoldering and he reeked of slaughter.

"Xerxes! King of Parsa and Mada, King of Bablyon and King of lands!" she greeted him, "Just who do you think you are?"

...to be continued

THE BOOK OF NEWS

★TORAHSCOPE★

BY
A CHALDEAN ASTROLOGER

Ephraim (Dec 22–Jan 19). Thou hast leadership potential, but a terrible temper. Thou gavest Gideon a hard time. Woe unto you this month!

Manasseh (Jan 20–Feb 18). Thou hast a split personality, and liveth on both sides of Jordan at once. Woe unto you this month, as well!

Benjamin (Feb 19–Mar 20). Thou art a survivor, although thou tendest to abuse other people's concubines. Woe unto you, for men shall call you "Benny" this month, and henceforth.

Reuben (Mar 21–Apr 19). Thou art naturally rebellious, and liketh the Dead Sea air. Because thou hast an unhealthy interest in thy father's concubine, thou shalt have a sandwich named after thee.

Simeon (Apr 20–May 20). Thou hast a wholly deserved inferiority complex, and messeth around with Edomites. This month, woe!

Judah (May 21–June 20). Though thou travelest much, and taketh many trips, thou art at heart a homebody,

and art also a survivor.

Issachar (June 21–Jul 22). Deep down, thou considerest thyself a prince, dost thou not? Woe unto thee this month!

Zebulun (Jul 23–Aug 22). Thou art very creative, and liketh to express thyself in writing; therefore, woe unto you!

Gad (Aug 23–Sept 22). Thou tendest to wake up in the morning on the wrong side of Jordan, dost thou not? Woe!

Asher (Sept 23–Oct 23). Thou art an incurable romantic, and tendeth to fall in love with false gôds. Unto you, therefore, woe!

Dan (Oct 24–Nov 21). Thou art very sensitive, and canst not abide Philistines. Thou shalt go on a long journey to the north, much to your woe.

Naphtali (Nov 22–Dec 21). Woe unto you this month, for thou hast a silly name, and no one hath ever heard of you.

"The Mystery of Evil."

*E*vil. Pain. Suffering. Tragedy. These are a Great Mystery. When we see, on our televisions, thousands starving in Africa, when we hear that a dear friend has cancer, or when we, personally, suffer a financial set-back, which of us has not asked that age-old theological Question: If God is Good, why is this happening to me?

"The finest minds in Christendom—St. Paul, St. Augustine, Martin Luther, Oral McJorrity, to name but a few—have meditated and prayed about this Mystery of Evil.

"And each of us has decided that God is Just. So whatever small inconvenience or hideous catastrophe befalls our fellow man, we can know, with the certainty of Faith, that It Served Him Right.

"Of course, that is the Message of Scripture. Whatever unspoken (and doubtless unspeakable) sins they committed, the Amorites, Moabites, Midianites, Caananites, Philistines, and inhabitants of Jabesh-gilead no doubt deserved to be massacred, man, woman, and child, by the Righteous Israelites.

"Now, the Book of the old so-called Bible that appears most explicitly to address the Mystery of Evil is Job.

"But the darn thing is 42 chapters long, and if you manage to stick with it right down to the "punchline," as it were, all you get is a lot of poetry about constellations and crocodiles!

"But our dedicated NOT THE BIBLE research team here at Oral State University © has, through a study of primary documents, succeeded in replicating the original facts in the case against Job, thereby confirming the Justice—nay, rather the MERCY—of God's actions. Job was asking for it."

GOD'S EYE ONLY

TOP SECRET

CRITICAL
CLASSIFIED

TOP SECRET

CLASSIFIED
GOD'S EYE ONLY

THE JOB PAPERS

PRELIM INTELLIGENCE DATA...EX IN-DEEP INVESTIGATION
COVERT PENETRATION...

SUBJECT: THY SERVANT JOB
CONTROL OIC: SATAN

FROM GOING TO AND FRO IN THE EARTH AND WALKING UP
AND DOWN IN IT, CONTROL OP "S" HAS (PER EXEC. OR-
DER) KEPT UNDER DIRECT SURVEILLANCE THY SERVANT
JOB. AGENCY HAS ASCERTAINED SUBJECT JOB ENGAGED
IN IMMORAL AND SUBVERSIVE ACTIVITIES CONSTITUTING
CLEAR AND PRESENT DANGER TO SECURITY, KINGDOM OF GOD.

POLITICAL DATA: (SUMMARY)

1. SUBJECT ALLEGEDLY "PERFECT AND UPRIGHT" CLAIMS UZ
CITIZENSHIP. IN FACT, IS JORDANIAN NATIONAL, PROB
EDOMITE, POSS CANANNITE SYMP. POSS LINKS PHILIS-
TINE LIBERATION ORGANIZATION.

2. SUBJECT IS SELF-CONFESSED SOCIALIST. DIRECT QUOTE
I WAS FATHER TO THE POOR, AND THE CAUSE WHICH I KNEW
NOT, I SEARCHED OUT UNQUOTE. (BUZZ WORDS "POOR" AND
"CAUSE" WELL-KNOWN CANAAN-SYMP CODE)

3. SUBJECT ADMITS MEMBERSHIP SECRET ORGANIZATIONS.
DQ I AM BROTHER TO DRAGONS AND A COMPANION OF
OWLS UQ. (BROTHERHOOD OF DRAGONS KNOWN AND INFIL-
TRATED MOAB-FRONT UNION...COMPANIONSHIP OF OWLS
HIGHLY SUSPECT SELF-STYLED SERVICE ORGANIZATION)

4. SUBJECT HAS AMASSED VAST PERSONAL WEALTH--EST
7000 SHEEP, 3000 CAMELS, 500 YOKE OF OXEN, 500 SHE-
ASSES. NO VISIBLE MEANS OF SUPPORT, REPORTED
SOURCES TAXABLE INCOME. *Why all she-asses?*
Poss use this? Double check. S.

5. AGENCY HAS REASON BELIEVE SUBJECT ENGAGED IN
SUBSTANTIAL AGRICULTURAL TRADE ACTIVITIES WITH
CHALDEANS AND SABEANS, BOTH INTERESTS HOSTILE
UNFRIENDLY TO MONOTHEISM.

RAW FILES...RAW FILES...RAW FILES...RAW FILES...

PERSONAL DATA:
(SUMMARY MATERIAL FROM DEEP-COVER HUMAN INTELLI-
GENCE SOURCES OPERATING AS "COMFORTERS" TO SUBJECT.
AGENTS E, Z, B)

1. STRONG EVIDENCE SUBJECT'S UNDUE SEXUAL ACTIVI-
TY...7 SONS, 3 DAUGHTERS. *Poss over-comp for homo?*
Dub-chek. S.

2. SUBJECT ADMITS STRONG "NUDIST" TENDENCIES.
DQ NAKED CAME I OUT OF MY MOTHER'S WOMB AND NAKED
SHALL I RETURN THITHER UQ.

3. SUBJECT ACTUALLY DIRECT-OBSERVED BY AGENTS E,
Z, B SITTING NAKED ATOP BACKYARD DUNG HEAP.
Poss copro? Dub-Chek. S.

4. NEIGHBORS REPORT SUBJECT'S DOMESTIC RELATIONS
STORMY. HEARD SUBJECT CALL WIFE DQ FOOLISH UQ.
WIFE CONSTANTLY URGES SUBJECT TO SUICIDE DQ CURSE
GOD AND DIE UQ.

5. ALL TEN SONS AND DAUGHTERS SWINGERS AND HABITUAL
DRUNKARDS. DRUG USE NOT VERIFIED. *Drug use not*
ruled out.
S.

6. SUBJECTS FREQUENT OVERSTATED DECLARATIONS OF
LOYALTY TO MONOTHEIST THEOCRATIC STATE EVALUATED
BY AGENTS E, Z, B TO BE INSINCERE, SUSPICIOUS,
TYPICAL EDOMITE.

RECOMMENDED ACTION: "OPERATION WHIRLWIND"

COMPANY PER EXECUTIVE ORDER TO UNDERTAKE NORMAL
FIVE-STAGE COUNTER-MEASURE AND RE-ORIENTATION
PROGRAM.

A) TERMINATE WITH EXTREME PREJUDICE ALL OFFSPRING
   OF SUBJECT.
B) UNDERTAKE FISCAL DESTABILIZATION AND CONFISCA-
   TORY ACTION RE: SHEEP, CAMELS, OXEN, SHE-ASSES.
   (poss. conduit friendly hostiles Chaldea, Sabea? S.)
C) BOTANICAL SUB. SEC. TO INFLICT SUBJECT WITH
   SORE BOILS.
D) EXPOSE SUBJECT IN-DEEP EXPERT INTERROGATION PER
   COL. ELIHU. MX PSYCH. AGON.
E) EXPOSE SUBJECT DIRECT PERSONAL CONTACT DIRECTOR.

Make a joyful no

How often does Holy Scripture admonish us to do this—
to sound a trumpet, pluck the harp, strike the tambour,
or raise our voice in song?

It would seem that

our very SOULS are in danger

of eternal torment if we do not heed God's holy commands—
and yet—
How few of us are gifted musically,
or even possess a trumpet
or tambour?

e unto the Lord!

Must we then PERISH?

No! There is yet hope!

Simply by acquiring, and playing at loud volume, this
collection of Sacred Music from Oral Sects Ltd©,
(not available in stores at any price)
you may yet be saved!
Yes, brothers and sisters, here they all are,
the Song of Solomon, the songs of King David,
and some original compositions by my faithful wife!
You'll hear the
Oral State University© **Tabernacle Choir**,
one thousand young white men and women singing your favorite
Negro Spirituals!
You'll thrill to such devotional tunes as
"In The Shade Of The Withered Fig Tree,"
"A Virgin Once Again," and
"A Flying Fortress Is Our God"!
And, if you order today, you'll receive, absolutely free,
a bonus recording of the McJorrity Family Singers©
rendering a selection from **Not The Bible**'s very own . . .

GOD'S GREATEST HITS!!

THE BOOK OF PSONGS

O Bloody, Bloody Jesus

He shall wash his feet in the blood of the wicked. (Ps 58: 10).

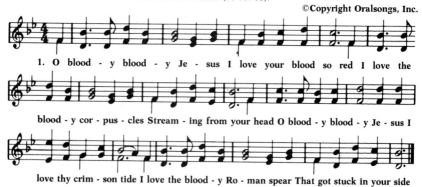

1. O blood - y blood - y Je - sus I love your blood so red I love the blood - y cor - pus - cles Stream - ing from your head O blood - y blood - y Je - sus I love thy crim - son tide I love the blood - y Ro - man spear That got stuck in your side

1. O bloody bloody Jesus
   I love your blood so red
   I love the bloody corpuscles
   Streaming from your head

2. O bloody bloody Jesus
   I love thy crimson tide
   I love the bloody Roman spear
   That got stuck in your side

3. O rare and bloody Jesus
   I love thy hands that bled
   I love the nails that pierced them
   O Jesus red and dead

4. I'd love to drink the blood O Lord
   That drips from off thy feet
   And wash my hands and brush my teeth—
   O Lord would that be sweet!

5. O bloody bloody Jesus
   I love thy blood so red
   I loved you when you were alive
   I love you better dead.

NOW Psalm 23 from the old so-called "Bible" is a beautiful piece of writing by God, as dictated to King David. It's *poetry*, in the very best sense of that word, which so often in our day means nothing more than plain Communist smut.

BUT for this time and place, it seemed to the scholars and translators at Oral State University © that the famous "pastoral" images, that is, references to sheep, were out of place. For as that Great Christian Gentleman, the late John Wayne, often observed, "This is cattle country."

WON'T you join us now, in singing along with this beautiful new version, which we like to call,

The Country and Western Psalm

He maketh them also to skip like a calf ... (Ps 29, 6).

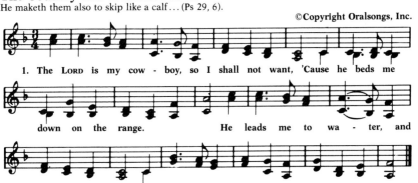

1. The LORD is my cow - boy, so I shall not want, 'Cause he beds me down on the range. He leads me to wa - ter, and he makes me drink, And he keeps me from get - tin' the mange.

    1.   The LORD is my cowboy, so I shall not want,
             'Cause he beds me down on the range.
             He leads me to water, and he makes me drink,
             And he keeps me from gettin' the mange.

    2.   We ride through the valley in the shadow of death
             From the rustlers who live in the hills,
             But I ain't scared, 'cause the LORD's ridin' high,
             And the touch of his spurs gives me chills.

    ch: The LORD is my cowboy, and I'm his cayuse
             Yipee-aye yipee-aye yipee-aay!
             And we'll come bye and bye to his Ranch up on high
             Where the skies are not cloudy all day.

    3.   The LORD is my cowboy, he feeds me his hay
             And he pours bucketsful in my trough.
             The LORD's in the saddle, the LORD's on my back,
             And I hope the LORD never gets off!

    ch: The LORD is my cowboy, and I'm his cayuse
             Yipee-aye yipee-aye yipee-aay!
             And we'll come bye and bye to his Ranch up on high
             Where the skies are not cloudy all day.

We Are Christian Warriors (militantly)

Thou hast broken the teeth of the ungodly ... (Ps 3: 7).

1. We are Chris - tian war - ri - ors, Sol - diers of the Lord! Right -
eous - ness our arm - or is, Vir - tue is our Sword! Meek - ness is
our ban - ner high, Char - i - ty our lance, ... etc.

1. We are Christian warriors,
   Soldiers of the Lord!
   Righteousness our armor is,
   Virtue is our Sword!
   Meekness is our banner high,
   Charity our lance,
   Chastity our battle ax
   And chain-mail iron pants!

2. We are Christian warriors,
   Brave and unafraid!
   Heathen foe shall fall before
   The force of our Crusade!
   Hark! Our trumpet summons men!
   Lo! Our ranks increase!
   We ride to Holy War behind
   The Mighty Prince of Peace!

3. We are Christian warriors,
   Merciless with Love!
   Innocently following
   Orders From Above!
   A Juggernaut, a Firestorm,
   A rising wrathful Tide!
   It's very fortunate for Him
   That God is on our side!

The Book of

PROVERBIAL WISDOM

SON, I sayeth, son, if thou wouldst get *wise* and have wisdom, incline thy ear to my words, and keep *shut* thy mouth;

For all the world honoreth wisdom, but *no one* liketh a guy which is wise.

If thou hast unto thyself thy health, *then* hast thou just about everything;

And wealth speaketh in a loud *voice*, but the dung of cattle walketh;

But if thou wouldst be accounted truly wise, then eat not in *any* place that calleth itself Mom's; nor shouldst thou *gamble* at cards with any man who is a physician;

And whosoever moveth his bowels in the self-same place where he breaketh his bread, is a fool.

Son, wouldst thou be accounted wise? Then get thyself *atop* the stick, and keep thou thine eyes upon the ball.

When thou goest unto a City, and *findeth* there a Hall, remember thou canst *not* fight it.

And forget not that a man must eat a *thousand* cubits of dung before he dieth;

But the wise man remembereth the side upon which his bread is *buttered*; and knoweth in his heart what is made when two is added unto *two*;

Be sharp, therefore, even as a tack *is* sharp, and forget not the law of thy fathers:

When thou hast them by the stones *of their loins*, the hearts of them will follow *thee*, and likewise their minds, also.

Go to woman, consider *her* ways; for thou canst not live without her, and neither canst thou live *with* her.

Son, I sayeth, son, that is a joke. Why laughest *thou* not?

Thine own bride shall be faithful and virtuous, and married in white *raiment*; but thy neighbors wife is an horse of a different *hue*.

For no man misseth a slice from a loaf *which* has been cut.

The fool sayeth in his heart, She is *too* old, or she is fat, or otherwise *uncomely*;

But the wise man knoweth *that* in the darkness, all cats are of the *self-same* hue, which *is* black.

Son, I sayeth son, am I going *too* fast for you?

The wise man knoweth which way the wind blowest, nor pisseth *he* into it.

When thou risest *up* in the assemblies to speak, *remember* the law of thy fathers:

Words are like *unto* the dung of cattle; and if thou flingest a *sufficiency thereof* at the side of a barn, doth not a goodly *portion* stick?

For I went forth and traveled far, and returned, and I *saw* under the sun that there is born *unto* us a sucker *every* minute.

My son, I sayeth, my son, if thou wouldst keep thy cookies *gathered* together and thy nethermost quarters *out* of a sling, remember the wisdom of thy father, who hath *been* around:

Such shekels as are *made* of wood, take them not.

Whatsover moveth, that thou *shalt* salute; but whatever moveth not, paint thou it.

And if the sister of thy mother, which is thy *aunt*, had stones upon her loins,verily, *then* wouldst she be thy uncle.

For the fool sayeth in the market place *that* winning is *everything*;

But the wise man knoweth *in his heart* that winning is the only thing.

The End.

Proverbial Wisdom!

Yes, friends, like so much of Holy Scripture, the Book of Proverbial Wisdom contains many of what I call "**Clichés to Live By**." But we here at **Oral's Sects© Inc.**, believe that **Divine Inspiration** is an on-going process, and have been moved by the Spirit to offer you, for a limited time only, these uplifting slogans for your home, office, torso, lapel, or back fender. Order today!

Guns Don't Kill People God Kills People!

"Thou shalt not touch that dial!"

ORAL

(CUE ORAL)

Hi there, Christians!

(USE THE SMILE)

I want to take this opportunity to say
a word about television.

(FROWN AND NOD)

A word of warning! Now don't get me
wrong. Television has been very good
to me. And very good to the Lord also.

(EYES UP, EYES DOWN)

Thanks to television, we down here at
KRIS-TV are able to bring you our
regular inspirational show, the very
lovely, very heartwarming hour of fire,
brimstone, and hymns: the 695 Club.

(THE SMILE AGAIN)

It's thanks to the 695 Club that you
good folks out there know where to
send all that money the Lord needs—for
future episodes of the 695 Club, for
the fine facilities over at Oral State,
and for the housing, transportation,
tennis courts and security systems
Christ will need when he returns.

(COUNT OFF FINGERS)

And of course, it's thanks to
television that we're able to let you
hungry Christians know about our new
chain of fast-food chapels, Beef 'n'
Pew, where in one easy stop, you can
chow down on a burger and offer up
a prayer.

(GAZE HEAVENWARD)

So hurry on down to our "Meatin' Place"!   (PAUSE, LEAN FORWARD
                                                   DO RIGHTEOUS WRATH
                                                   LOOK)

But these are the moral uses of
television. Elsewhere in the so-called
"media" what do we find? Sex! Crime!
Drugs! Racy language! News! Often
when my faithful wife and I are watching
TV, we're forced to wear blindfolds and
ear stopples to prevent this filth from
entering our minds! Now, they say we're
free to change channels! That's not
freedom, that's slavery! And whatever
we may think of slavery in principle,
in this particular case, it's contrary
to the Will of God!   (PAUSE, VERY QUIET)

But say we do change the channel, and
on this new channel there's some
wholesome Christian show like the 695
Club, which now appears daily on over
350 stations—check your local listings?   (START TO BUILD)

What happens to that other channel we
switched from? Does it "go away"?
Does it "cease to exist"? NO!! It's
still there in the TV, spreading its
filth and Godlessness, stinking up the
insides of our Home Entertainment
Center!! Why, it's almost as if that
TV was a sinner like you and you!   (RAISE FIST)

Let me speak to you from the heart,
my friends.

(THROW AWAY NOTES)

Our TVs have got to be born-again!
Our TVs have got to be purged of
sin and filth so that they, too,
can enter the kingdom of Heaven!

(DO THE SMILE)

For what's the kingdom of Heaven
going to be like without a little
TV? As always, the Bible has an
answer. Long ago, before there
were fabulous shows like the 695
Club, people got their inspirations
from visions! Mostly these <u>visions</u>
came directly from God—just like
the 695 Club—but sometimes people
got "tuned" to the wrong "channel."
And that "channel" was the "channel
of Satan"! People had visions of
filth and Godlessness right there
in their own heads!

(DO INSPIRATIONAL
SMILE, HEAD TO
ONE SIDE)

But the prophet of the Lord saw into
their heads, my friends, and he urged
them—before it was too late—to <u>ban</u>
the visions of Satan, and turn back
to the programming of God. His words
although more than two thousand years
old, have an important message for us
today. So don't touch that dial! I'll
be right back after THE BOOK OF VISIONS!

The Book of
VISIONS

The People Watcheth Smut

1 These are the words of the LORD which came unto his prophet concerning the abominations of His people, and the dirt of their *minds*, and the filth of their *visions*:

2 Woe unto you My people, for you do *wallow* in visions of iniquity; fornication filleth your heads and your eyeballs are of *dung*; yea, like the apples of the road are *your* eyeballs;

3 From morning *even* unto night ye sit like whores in an *whore*-house; and Mine enemies, Satan *and* his gang cometh unto ye like them that come *unto* whores; and they do enter into your bodies through the eye-*sockets* and rot your minds *with* their filth!

4 And the reflection of their lewdness is *upon* your foreheads, oh whores, and the hot breath of their transmissions is upon your cheeks! Yet that which whores trade for an stiff *price*, ye givest *away* for free! Yea, some of ye even *pay* for visions!

5 Woe unto ye my people. For the air of My land is polluted thereby; and the snowiness of thy bodies is darkened; and Mine enemies do prosper and *remain* unbombed. I say *unto* ye, saith the LORD, That unless ye become as blind *men* to these visions, my curse shall come upon ye!! Worms shall eat thy eyeballs, *and* My foot shall tread *on* thy heads and cause thy corrupted brains to ooze from the holes *therein* like paste of the tooth!

6 I have revealed a vision *unto ye*, continueth the LORD. A vision of Heaven; it is regularly scheduled, and each week is it revealed to ye and yet do ye shun it, and its ratings *stinketh*;

7 From angelic choirs all clothed in white, do ye *turn* away, and from mountains of flowers *that* perish not, and from pure women that are without the appeal of *sex* and from the mighty organ that *is in* the vault of My Place; from singing and praising Me unto all eternity with joyous hymns and bright instruments do ye turn away, and from sending checks and money orders to My prophet!

8 Woe unto ye my people, that knoweth not a good vision when ye *see* it!

Concerning Dug-Jiggling

9 Woe unto ye whose visions are of harlots who do cover their dugs with tops that are called *bi-ki'ni*; and who at the dropping of an cue do break into a trot or drive over rocky ground, so that their dugs *jiggleth*! For lo, I made dugs to *give suck* not *jiggle*!

10 Jiggling dugs *are* an abomination in My sight!

11 I shall cast those dug-jiggling harlots and them who behold them into everlasting fire and their dugs *shall* be sucked for all eternity! For that they have filled me with wrath, I might *even* suck them Myself, addeth the LORD.

12 And woe unto them whose visions are of Nubians running *around* all over the *place* and being sassy! For though there be good Nubians, yet have I made them *to be* hewers of wood and drawers of water and shiners of shoe-leather. Respectfulness have I given unto the Nubian and a good set of pipes; look ye *to* My vision and ye shall behold good Nubians. Respectful and neatly clad are they, and singing up *a storm*!

13 And unto them whose visions include Nubian *harlots*, woe a thousand fold! For who in My world *wanteth* to see a pair of *Nubian* dugs *jiggling*?

Speaking of Nubians

14 And speaking of Nubians, saith the LORD, Why are ye so taken in thy visions with them as smoketh white powders and injecteth weeds into their bodies? *Huh*? Such are *but* garbage on *two* legs, and shall be compacted and cast into the incinerator *of* my wrath! Yet when I walk about in the earth privily, beholding the visions of My people, weeds and white powders *abound* therein! Nor is it just Nubians which commit such abominations but Mine own people and the fruits of their loins. And some of these fruits are barely the age of teen!

15 Double *woe* unto them whose visions show the officers of My Law in a bad light; and double-double *woe* unto them as show Mine officers clowning and fooling. For these men put their lives on the line for Me each day, and unto them have I given My Law; (Yet to be fair, saith the LORD, some visions have I beheld, *concerning* the officers of My Law, which are alright in My Sight. It particularly pleaseth Me when some punk rapist consumeth a bellyful of hot lead with no questions asked).

16 But woe unto them with visions of sodomites who *do* prance *and* dance, for the buttocks thereof are the seat of sin;

17 And woe to them whose vision doth slant the news *from afar*, so that it looketh as if Mine enemies *are* winning; yea, woe unto *them* who do behold interviews *with* Mine enemies, for why *giveth* them the airtime?

18 Seek ye to deceive the LORD God? exclaimeth the LORD in amazement. Are ye *crazy*! For My Vision is infinite and *My* Surveillance perpetual!

Them that Have Cable

19 But *most* of all, woe unto them which *do* have visions after midnight. For after midnight, when My People ought to be in bed asleep with their

hands outside *the* sheet, then are such abominations beheld, that even the face of the LORD thy God turneth red *with shame.* Verily I say unto ye, although I created all which is in heaven *and* earth, yet that which happeneth *after* midnight was made by *Someone Else.*

20 What happeneth therein stoppeth the mouth *of* the Almighty; yet let Me *just* say, that while I madeth dugs to be sucked and not to jiggle, yet never were they to be sucked by a . . .

21 I cannot go on, saith the LORD.

22 YEA, DESTRUCTION SHALL RAIN DOWN UPON THEM WITH NOCTURNAL VISIONS! Abominations are they, may their limbs and seed wither! Filthy and foul are the minds of My people, saith the LORD, *and* their heads are my *restroom!*

23 *Ban* ye these visions, thundereth the LORD, boycott them who do *send* them *into* your heads; String ye them up who bawleth about freedom of speech and burn ye the sign of My Son (which is to come) upon *their* lawns! For they are as leper's *lips* unto Me; like body odor are they in My Nose; unworthy are they to dwell *in* My Armpit.

24 Yet am I just, goeth on the LORD *more* quietly, and throwing away *His* Notes; I understandeth the needs of My People. For lo, they need entertainment at the end of their *day's* labor; and their wives *need* something while their men are at labor, to keep *their* minds from lewdness;

25 *Therefore*—ye shall have a Vision O My People, from dawn even unto the end of the prime of time; and it shall be wholesome, and pure and pleasing to Me and to My Prophet; It shall *be* My Authorized Vision, And it shall go something like this:

The Authorized Vision

7:00 GOOD MORNING ASSYRIA (Cohorts, gleaming in purple and gold descendeth upon the Host)

9:00 SHIBBOLETH STREET (Counting sheep. Counting Goats. Telling the difference)

10:00 LET'S MAKE A COVENANT (R)

11:00 THE CHOSEN PEOPLE'S COURT (A custody battle. Solomon presideth)

12:00 ZION'S HOPE (Tamar telleth *her* brother Absolom what *his* brother Amnon did)

1:00 ALL HIS CHILDREN (Samson thinketh that he's found Miss Right. She's a hair-dresser)

2:30 GIDEON'S ISLAND (R)

3:00 ADAM'S FAMILY (R)

3:30 WIDE WORLD OF SPIRITS (A look back at the Galloping Ghost; a study of the Phantom Double Play; Doctor Dunkenstein performeth several total immersions)

6:00 THAT'S CREDIBLE! (This even, a man who can knock down walls with the blowing of a trumpet; Moses getteth water from a rock; and an interview with one who claimeth to have spent three days inside a whale!)

6:30 HOLY DAYS (His fellow students at Philistine High maketh fun of Ritchie's circumcised member. Fonzie taketh them out back for a *bris* with a breadknife)

7:00 ALL IN THE HOLY FAMILY (His mother giveth Meathead a big 30th birthday party; but step-dad Joe spoileth the fun by suggesting he get a job)

7:30 THREE'S TRINITY (The maidens of Galilee run for cover when the Holy Ghost hitteth town, and all heaven breaketh loose)

8:00 THE GOD COUPLE (R)

9:00 WAY UPSTAIRS, WAY DOWNSTAIRS (Hijinx in Paradise have infernal repercussions, when Lucifer refuseth to serve)

10:00 LOVE ARK (All those "two-by-two" animals starteth to give Noah ideas. Guest heavenly bodies: Elizabeth Taylor and Orson Welles, as "Mr and Mrs. Behemoth")

11:00 SABBATH NIGHT LIVE (Guest host: The LORD God of Hosts; Elijah and his performing ravens. Musical guest: The Cleft Stones)

12:00 (Midnight) In bed, asleep, with hands outside the sheets. Thus spake the LORD unto His Prophet

THE ORAL EXAMINATION©

Examine me, O LORD, and prove me; try my reins and my heart.   (Ps 26, 2)

Examine yourselves, whether ye be in the faith...   (II Cor. 13, 5)

Do not begin examination until told to do so!

THE ORAL EXAMINATION©

Here is a short multiple choice quiz, based on the Oral State University©
entrance examination, to test *your* personal knowledge of Scripture.

Candidates answering all questions correctly, and/or making a sufficient
Love Offering to the Oral State University© Scholarship Fund will
receive an honorary Doctorate of Divinity, which entitles them to:
a) lobby vociferously for a larger Defense Budget and   **b)** not pay
any Income Tax

a b
|| ||

GENESIS:
According to Divinely Inspired and Literal Biblical figures, Methuselah
was born 687 years after Adam—that is, in the year 3317 B.C., and
lived 969 years; that is, until the year 2348 B.C.
The flood, which occurred when Methuselah's grandson Noah was
600 years old, can be unerringly dated to the year 2448 B.C. Thus
Methuselah lived 100 years after the flood. Methuselah survived the
flood by:
a) treading water?   **b)** holding his breath?   **c)** disguising himself
aboard the ark as an old goat?

a b c
|| || ||

EXODUS:
After crossing the Red Sea, Moses and the Israelites turned *right*:
a) because a guided tour of the Sinai was part of the package?
b) out of a poor sense of direction?   **c)** for deeply meaningful political reasons?

a b c
|| || ||

LEVITICUS:
One of the following creatures is edible, according to the LORD God.
a) The rabbit?   **b)** The pig?   **c)** The lobster?   **d)** The beetle?

a b c d
|| || || ||

NUMBERS:
In "the matter of Peor" (Num. 31:16) Moses, acting according to the
LORD's commands:
a) Slew the kings of Midian and all the males and took the spoil of
their cattle and all their flocks and burnt all their cities?   **b)** Slew the
kings of Midian and all the males and took the spoil of their cattle and
all their flocks and burnt all their cities and killed all the women and
children?   **c)** Slew the kings of the Midian and all the males and
took the spoil of their cattle and all their flocks and burnt all their cities
and killed all the women and male children, but kept the women
children alive for themselves?

a b c
|| || ||

DEUTERONOMY:
"Thou shalt not lend upon usury to thy brother; usury of money, usury
of victuals, usury of anything that is lent upon usury" (Deut. 23:19).
Here and elsewhere (Exod. 22:25; Ps. 15:5; Prov. 28:8; and Ezek.
18:13;) the LORD God prohibits and condemns this abominable practice of "usury." Usury means:
a) Having cream in your coffee while eating a hamburger?   **b)** Having
sex with the woman on top?   **c)** Something else?

a b c
|| || ||

JOSHUA:
Draw a map of Israel based on the detailed instructions in Joshua, chapters 12 to 22. Contemplate it. Does it portend:
a) The fulfillment of the prophesies? **b)** The Second Coming? a b c
c) Lower oil prices? || || ||

JUDGES:
Everyone knows that Abimelech, who judged Israel twenty and three years and then died (Judg. 10:1-2) was the grandson of Dodo. But was his father named: a b c
a) Puah? **b)** Kanga? **c)** Eeyore? || || ||

RUTH:
Ruth, Naomi's daughter-in-law and the grandmother of King David (from whose line Christ Himself descended), was *not* an Israelite, but a *Moabite*. (Ruth 1:4). This proves:

a) The Book of Ruth, perhaps the most beautiful story in all the Old Testament, is apocryphal? **b)** The Bible is not the inspired and a b c
unerring Word of God? **c)** Jesus was not really Jewish? || || ||

SAMUEL:
When the Philistines stole the ark, God "smote the men . . . and they had emerods in their secret parts" (1 Sam 5:9), and when they returned the ark, it contained five gold emerods (1 Sam 6:17). Symbolically speaking, this means:
a) Dagon, god of the Philistines, was a false god? **b)** The LORD God was with Samuel, who was judge over Israel? **c)** Philistines a b c
frequently have piles of gold? || || ||

KINGS:
Solomon "had seven hundred wives, princesses and three hundred concubines" (1 Kings 11:3). Yet his son, Rehoboam, said, "My little *finger* shall be thicker than my father's loins." (1 Kings 12:10). This explains:
a) The hasty departure of the Queen of Sheba? **b)** Solomon's obsession with cedar beams? **c)** How Rehoboam came to sunder a b c
in twain the kingdoms of Israel and Judah? || || ||

CHRONICLES:
"Jehoiachin *was* eight years old when he began to reign . . . ?nd he did *that which* was evil in the sight of the LORD." (2 Chron. 36:9). It is likely Jehoiachin committed the abomination of:
a) Ahab? **b)** Onan? **c)** It's a misprint, and he actually was eigh- a b c
teen years old, (see 2 Kings 24:8)? || || ||

EZRA/NEHEMIAH:
With these books, the ten tribes of Israel are lost, and the story of Israel is ended, although the story of the "Jews" (i.e. Judeans) continues. Thus, the Inspired Word of God proves:
a) God broke his promise to Abraham? **b)** The Judeans were the *true* children of Abraham? **c)** It is possible to be strongly pro-Israeli, a b c
and still dislike Jews? || || ||

ESTHER:
Queen Vashti refuses to do the bidding of her husband King Ahasuerus. He throws her out. This event establishes:

a) That the story is an ancient Persian fairy tale? **b)** That the story is a political allegory, Vashti being an epynom for India, Ahasuerus for Persia? **c)** That we should vote "No" on E.R.A.?

a b c
|| || ||

JEREMIAH:
Fill in the blanks:
(Jer. 13:11). "For as the _____ cleaveth to the _____ of a man, so have I caused to cleave unto me the whole house of Israel and the whole house of Judah, saith the LORD."

LAMENTATIONS OF JEREMIAH:
Fill in the blanks:
(Lam. 1:9). "Her _____ *is* in her _____; she remembereth not her last end."

ESSAY QUESTION:
In 100 words or less, compare the sublime imagery of Jeremiah the Prophet with the gutter-minded smut in so much of today's so-called "satire."

EZEKIEL:
"Woe to the *women* that sew pillows to all arm holes" (Ezek. 13:18). Here and elsewhere the LORD God speaks out against this practice which "Makes souls to fly." Thus we are warned against:

a) False gods? **b)** False prophets? **c)** Other?

a b c
|| || ||

DANIEL:
Before being cast into the den of lions, Daniel had subsisted for years on a diet of "pulse" (Dan. 1:16). The lions totally avoided Daniel, and he was delivered. "Pulse" is:

a) Milk and honey? **b)** Bread and water? **c)** Beans?

a b c
|| || ||

HOSEA:
"And Jacob fled into the country of Syria, and Israel served for a wife, and for a wife kept he *sheep*." (Hos. 12:12). Bearing in mind that by "Israel" the prophet here means Abraham, the passage means:

a) Abraham was Jacob's wife? **b)** Both sheep and Abraham were Jacob's wives? **c)** Abraham was a sheep?

a b c
|| || ||

THE END OF THE GOOD OL' TESTAMENT

"And now..."

THE NEO-TESTAMENT

Thus we come to the End of an Era, the final days of the "Covenant," or "New Deal" between God and the Israelites.

"For over 4000 years, His original "Chosen People," that is, the Jews, carelessly squandered God's bountiful Reserves of Grace, spending and wasting His store of Mercy as if it were infinite. They sinned, repented, and backslid again and again, in a Wages-of-Sin/Price-of-Salvation spiral, all while issuing countless books by minor prophets; printing, as it were, devalued paper, against the long-depleted Patience of the Lord God.

"By the year 1 B.C. the Jews were morally and spiritually bankrupt.

"Clearly, it was time for a New Beginning—time for one Man to accept a Mandate—to get the People back to work, praying hard, saving and being saved, earning Grace the old fashioned way. It was time for a Man who would get mankind's spiritual economy back on the Supply Side.

"And that Man was Jesus Christ.

"The story of Jesus occupies no fewer than four "Gospels" in the old so-called New Testament. Yet not a one of them makes more than a passing reference to the first thirty years of Christ's life!

"Why?

"Could it be that those who have meddled with and corrupted Holy Scripture down the years didn't want us to know what kind of kid Christ was—what sort of pupil, what manner of young man? Perhaps it was their wish to keep us in the dark concerning the good old-fashioned Values His parents instilled in Him, and the gratitude He showed them, by Clean Living and a Positive Attitude.

"Here, then, is the simple but inspiring story of a young Man we all admire very much, and from whom each and every one of us can learn a great deal.

"Could we have a very warm, very pious welcome for:"

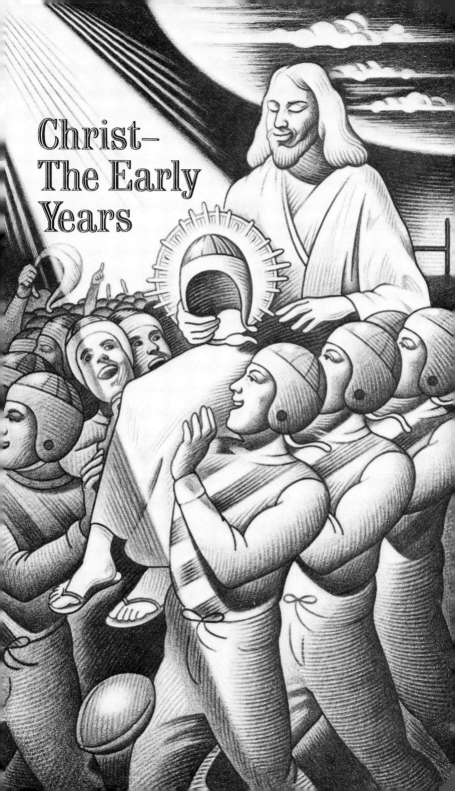

Christ–
The Early
Years

"It's a boy!" squealed Mary excitedly.

Joseph nodded affirmatively.

"It certainly is, Mary," he said contentedly. "There's no doubt about it," he added admiringly.

They kissed carefully.

Things had not been easy for the bright, cheerful, desperately poor young couple. Just nine months before, Joseph, 22, had married Mary, 18. He was a carpenter and she was a virgin. On their wedding night Mary told Joseph she was pregnant and that the father was God. Burning doubts filled Joseph's mind, which he easily stifled. But others whispered wicked things about Mary. They spread rumors that she had been engaging in premarital sex. Some even urged her to have a federally funded abortion, which is nothing more than downright murder. Imagine where we'd be today, if Mary had heeded their sinful words!

"Hi!" shouted a rough voice chummily. "We're shepherds!"

"And we're three kings!" boomed foreign voices deeply. "We were guided by the star," one continued in his heavily accented English. Mary looked outside. Over the lowly stable where they had been callously housed by the unfeeling inn-keeper, hung a huge star, suspended in the sky, as bright as day.

"Gee Joe," sighed the young woman blissfully. "Isn't this exciting? I'm so glad I'm the mother of God!" she averred warmly.

"And his wife!" was Joseph's playful retort.

Their visitors, both mighty and humble, seemed to sense there was something special about the baby, for they fell to their knees and began worshipping Him. The three kings had also brought Him presents and some gold. The latter Mary and Joseph refused to accept. Despite their grinding poverty, both Christs were of the opinion that hand-outs only encourage laziness and crime.

The presents, though, were another matter and these they accepted with alacrity. The royal gifts were (a) frankincense, an aromatic gum resin yielded by trees of the genus Boswellia, and (b) myrrh, which is much the same thing.

Their guests having left, Joseph and Mary themselves had to make a hurried departure. King Herod of Judea, where the young couple were staying, had ordered the police to kill all children two-years-old and younger in the land. Thanks to a dream, the happy parents got wind of this and fled to Egypt immediately. Later they returned and settled down in the sleepy little village of Nazareth. Joseph and Mary always raised their "son" according to the word of God. For instance after Mary married God, an Angel had visited her and told her that God wanted His boy called Jesus. But when Mary took her new baby to be christened, the priest objected, saying that Jesus was not a Jewish name. (This was when the Christs were still Jews). The priest wanted her to pick a normal Jewish name like Saul, David, or Herman. But Mary insisted. She knew that you don't question the word of God. After all, when the Angel had told her to call her child Jesus, she too had objected.

"But that's a Spanish name," she had quavered faintly.

The Angel's face had clouded with anger.

"So is Angel!" came the thunderous reply.

Poor though they were, the Christs worked hard. For them lack of money was no excuse for shabbiness and junk food. So Jesus always had decent clothes, and regular nourishing meals. He grew up a healthy virile young animal, mischievous, clear-eyed, thoughtful, tall, generous, obedient, neat, kind to animals, and athletic. His sturdy physique and rippling well-developed muscles stood Him in good stead in the daily contests of strength and agility between the boys of Nazareth. These competitions arose from high spirits and youthful energy, rather than the desire to see others lose, and Jesus won them constantly. But He would never have dreamed of using His superior strength to take advantage of another boy, or to "show off" or to "beat him to a pulp."

Unless of course, He was forced to.

Judas was the son of a rich money-changer who lived in a large house in the expensive section of Nazareth. He was jealous of Jesus' popularity with the other boys, for the Son of God was a natural leader and His blonde hair picked Him out from among His darker-complexioned fellows. Judas was always taunting Jesus, supporting His opponents in their friendly bouts of wrestling and smiting, and using sarcasm. But Jesus always took the razzing good-naturedly, and employed His ready wit to turn the joke back on the sallow youth. This only made the malcontent more envious, and one day He went too far. Jesus had just won a wrestling bout with a clean pin. Laughingly He helped up his burly adversary, who was rubbing his head ruefully.

From the circle of admirers came the sarcastic observation:

"Probably some dirty truck He learned from His 'father'!"

Jesus flushed hotly. His blue eyes glinted hardly.

"Withdraw those words, Judas," he said tightly, for it was Judas who had spoken.

"Why? Everyone knows your father's just a dirty old carpenter from Egypt! Anyway, he's not your father!"

Even though this was true, Jesus' jaw set grimly. This was no time for wit. (While He cared nothing for Himself, the honor of his poverty-stricken but hardworking parents must be upheld.)

"Those are fighting words, Judas, but I'm giving you one last chance to eat them," gritted the Boy through clenched teeth.

"Huh!" was the mocking rejoinder. "A coward as well as a sissy!" added the olive-skinned Judas, referring to Jesus' blonde hair.

Sensing trouble the other boys had drawn away. This was what Judas had been waiting for. Without their close scrutiny, he could use low blows, kicks and other unsporting tricks—just the sort of cheating he'd accused Jesus of! Intending to make short work of Jesus, the richer of the two boys, who was also taller and heavier, charged confidently. At the last moment, however, Jesus sidestepped neatly. A punishing left connected with Judas' jaw, followed by a crisp right. Bemused, the bully shook his head, spewing out a veritable hail of broken teeth.

"Now you've nothing to eat those words with," taunted Jesus quietly. "I guess I'll have to force them down your throat!"

Judas swung wildly. Jesus hooked coolly: once, twice, thrice! His opponent's brilliantined head came down. Now was the time for the knock-out . . . but Jesus held back.

"Just retract your foul words," He urged calmly. "And we'll call it quits."

"OK," muttered the bully through bleeding lips and proffered his hand. Trustingly Jesus grasped it, and suddenly found Himself yanked into a spine-cracking bear-hug. Judas had tricked Him! Jesus had no choice now but to teach the bully a lesson. Reluctantly He jerked His knee into Judas' groin, and, fists whirling, quickly reduced the spoiled youth's face to a bleeding pulp. Judas went down. Much against his will, Jesus ground His heel repeatedly into the miscreant's limp form. Mercifully the pampered boy's ribs cracked easily. The other boys cheered. The richly deserved lesson in respect was over.

Jesus' best friend was His second cousin, John the Baptist. Mr. and Mrs. Baptist had been very old when they had John, and had soon died, leaving him all alone in the world. He lived by himself beside the River Jordan, and eked out a precarious existence, polishing sandals and performing other small services. The good people of Nazareth, including Joseph and Mary, who were his relatives, did not really approve of John and regarded him as an undesirable. (And it must be said that they had a point, for John was far from a model boy—his appearance alone left much to be desired). Jesus, however, knew that fending for oneself can be a great molder of character. He was certain that some day John would achieve greatness, and the two were inseparable.

Boys will be boys, of course, and John and Jesus often got into hot water. Once they decided to run away. They built a raft and sailed off down the River Jordan. They camped and had a fine old time. Soon it grew dark and Jesus began to think about His parents, while John, who had none, didn't. Jesus decided to leave His companion and make His way home. It took a whole day and what should he find going on in Nazareth when He arrived, but His own funeral! Was his face red! As was His backside, for despite His being descended from God, Joseph whupped him soundly.

On another occasion when Jesus stayed away from home, though, Joseph's strap was not in evidence. Jesus went to school in Jerusalem and got excellent grades. This was no surprise for the lad was industrious, hardworking, and keen. Jesus had to walk to Jerusalem every day, for there was no transportation to the school, nor did the Christs expect any. One night He didn't come home, nor the next, nor the next. Perplexed and worried His "parents" set out to find Him. Imagine their amazement when they got to Jerusalem and there was Jesus, sitting in school, surrounded by His teachers! While they were harboring suspicions of His having run away, their "son" had actually been studying for three straight days and nights! Now *their* faces were red! Mary went up to Jesus and asked Him what he was doing. Prophetically the Stripling replied:

"Don't you know I must be about my Father's business? And that the business of my Father *is* business?"

When Jesus said "Father" He meant God, of course. Mary on the other hand, thought He meant Joseph, which is hardly surprising when you consider that she had only met God once, many years before and for a very short while. In any case her mistake gave her a great idea.

Why not send Jesus to college? Not only would this give Him all the advantages higher education can bring in later life, but He could learn advanced skills and help Joseph in his struggling carpentry business.

Her "husband" and his "son" agreed enthusiastically, and before long Jesus was a familiar sight on the small, bustling campus of Galilee Community College. Knowing the sacrifices Joseph and Mary were making, Jesus studied hard at His minor, Advanced Carpentry, and His major, Business Administration. But the true love of the tall, strapping blonde young Son of God was sports.

As we have seen, Jesus was a natural athlete. But as He had not had the advantage of attending a school with an extensive athletic program, He knew little of team sports. He was all thumbs, He fumbled the ball, He misread signals. After the game, His team-mates ignored Him, but the coach approached Him in the locker room.

"Jesus, you were awful!" said the older man, quietly. "But you've got pluck and spirit. Practice hard, learn the ropes, live clean, and I'll give you another chance."

That night, the youth vowed He would make the team or die trying. He knew that deep within Him, slept the will of an indomitable champion. All that year, without neglecting His studies, He trained furiously. The distractions of smoking, drinking and consorting with girls were not for him; every spare moment He could find He kicked, caught, ran, relentlessly hammering His young body into a rock-hard machine of muscle and stamina.

Of course being God, He could have made the team easily if He'd wanted. But using His omnipotence in so sneaky a manner would have seemed to Jesus perilously close to cheating.

His determination paid off. The following fall, at the very first try-out, Jesus was the sensation of the gridiron. Time and again the pitiless body of Christ smashed through the defense; time and again the greedy hands of the Son of God pierced the ozone for another impossible catch. By dusk that chilly fall evening, Galilee had a new champion. All through the season, Jesus went from strength to strength. The local scribes took much interest in the new star, chronicling His triumphs with glee. There was only one cloud on the young athlete's horizon, and that was His old rival, Judas.

Judas played on the Galilee team. He had a good turn of speed especially when being chased, but was loath to tackle or be tackled. Naturally He was jealous of Jesus, and this jealousy almost destroyed the team. It was the eve of the big game between Galilee and their arch-enemies, Pharisee U. Strict curfew was ordered for the Galilee squad. But Judas, who had a weakness for drink and women, decided to sneak out to a local tavern and get drunk. He was removed by the police but not before one of the local scribes had recognized him. Having bought the silence of the officers Judas made his way back to his dorm and fell into a troubled sleep.

The next morning, the local chronicle carried a sarcastic story about "a certain player" and his training methods. The coach called the team together and demanded to know who was responsible. Judas remained silent. The coach had no option but to search every man's locker, and when he did so, several empty bottles were found in Our Hero's locker.

Judas had placed them there earlier to avoid blame for his immoral behavior! Jesus, being God, knew Judas to be the culprit, yet He could not tattle on a team-mate. When the coach told Him He was benched, His firm young jaw set in a grim line.

The big game was a disaster. Without Jesus, Galilee could not hold back their arch-rivals. Time and again the pitiless Pharisees smashed through the Galilee line; time and again, hungry Pharisee hands plucked the pigskin from the hapless Galileans. Jesus watched disconsolately. He could not believe that Judas would betray the team for his own selfish ends.

It was deep in the fourth quarter. Suddenly Jesus heard a whining voice at his elbow. "Say, killer, how come you're warming the bench?" It was the scribe who had written the sarcastic story.

Jesus would say nothing. Dark suspicion furrowed the scribe's brow. "Does the Coach think you're the one I wrote about?" he cried incredulously.

Still Jesus' jaw clamped shut. The scribe, however, scenting a new and better story, turned to Judas, who was coming off the field after another twenty-yard loss. "Hey handsome," he shrilled, "how's the hangover?"

Judas' face drained chalkily. The coach's eyes narrowed shrewdly.

Judas' deception had finally caught up with him!

"Turn in your jersey, Judas!" clenched the coach between gritted teeth.

"Jesus, get out there—and save us!"

Only a miracle could beat the Pharisees now, and that afternoon Jesus performed miracles. Time and again the boulder-like Son of God smashed through waves of Pharisee defenders; time and again, His point-starved palms snatched the leather from Pharisee fingers. With ten seconds to go, Galilee was still four points behind. Jesus sped downfield for one final desperate pass. Four Pharisees covered Him like a second skin. Of course, He could have turned them into dust, but that would have been wrong. What He had to do was make a super-human effort, jump as He'd never jumped before!

He leapt! The ball was His! The huge Pharisees tore at His limbs. But the oak-like legs would not be denied the goal-line! He was over! He had scored! He had saved Galilee!

But the manly pleasure Jesus took in His hard-earned victory, was nothing to the inner joy He experienced upon His graduation. The ill-concealed delight of His parents radiated from their shining faces. Now He had the skills to repay their tremendous sacrifices, and within a very short time, the dynamic young man was putting theory into practice.

One fateful day, Jesus was sitting in Joseph's carpentry shop, whittling away at a wooden peg. The peg, when completed, would be used to connect two boards in which Joseph was boring holes. Suddenly the younger man threw down his work.

"Dad!" he exclaimed, "I've got an idea!"

"Fire away 'son,'" rejoined his "father" distractedly, still working laboriously on the second hole.

"Metal's harder than wood, right?" demanded Jesus. He hurried on impatiently. "So if we sharpened a small piece of metal we could bang it into wood, correct?" He continued without waiting for a reply. "And if we banged it through two boards, they'd hold together, wouldn't they?"

He seized the two boards from the carpenter's unwilling hands and turned His words to deeds with a nearby hammer. He handed the result to His skeptical onlooker. The two boards seemed to be tightly fastened by the sharpened piece of metal. Would they hold? They did! Try as he could, the grizzled craftsman could not pry them asunder. Jesus had discovered nails!

Nails were the turning point for the Christ family. Thanks to His training, Jesus knew that it was not enough to have a good idea. In order to maximize its potential, one must promote it aggressively. Nails cut Joseph's production time in half, enabling him to move up delivery schedules and beat out the competition. Orders poured in. In fact there were many more than Joseph could handle. But did Jesus turn down those orders? Of course not! He thought big, He thought expansion. Why not, said Jesus, open a whole chain of carpentry shops, with a reliable image, and exclusive rights to nails, then lease them to independent operators for a fixed monthly fee?

All they needed was a catchy name. Outside his shop, Joseph had erected a sign which read: "J. Christ and 'Son' Carpenters." One evening, he noticed it had been taken down. The next morning, Jesus displayed the new sign. It showed Jesus and Joseph in carpenters' aprons, holding hammers and nails, ready for work. Above their heads was the proud legend:

TWO GUYS FROM NAZARETH

Enterprising carpenters, anxious to get their hands on nails, bought Jesus' idea one hundred percent. Throughout Galilee, "Two Guys from Nazareth" signs mushroomed overnight. Of course, Jesus and Joseph weren't actually working in the shops; in fact they never had to lift a hammer again; but they sold all the nails, received the fixed monthly fee, and hired a good lawyer to deal with complaints. In a few short weeks, through initiative, and a razor-sharp business sense, Jesus had both revolutionized carpentry and invented franchising!

With the senior Christs on the road to riches, Jesus could afford to turn His attention to other matters. For some time, the Son of God had had the feeling that there was something missing. At first He thought the answer was girls. At school, He had had nothing to do with girls, seeing them as a threat to His athletic prowess, His health and good name. Many of His so-called friends had urged the handsome blonde young giant to date girls, kiss them goodnight and even go further, but fortunately Jesus had been able to resist these tempters, and now at the age of 25 He still felt clean and whole.

No, the answer was not girls. If God wanted His Son to marry and settle down, He would send along Miss Right soon enough. There was no need to "experiment," to "explore relationships," to jeopardize his eternal soul for a few moments of dubious pleasure in a darkened vehicle. Perhaps the answer lay in renewed business activity. He had clearly been given the gift of making money. Should He not put that gift to work for his own and others' benefit?

For several years Jesus threw Himself into work with a vengeance. With excess capital from the Two Guys from Nazareth Corp., Jesus made many shrewd investments in such areas as farming, health-care, commodities, and national defense, all of which provided Him with invaluable tools later in life, in communicating with the most responsible and most powerful elements of society. He never of course used His divine gift of foresight to manipulate, say, the stock market, or other speculative ventures, for this would have been unethical. He did, however, finance various charities—for example purchasing the inn where He had been born, and setting up a permanent facility for young impoverished couples. Never again would a Son of God have to be born in the filth and noise of a common stable. (He also made sure that the callous innkeeper was dismissed, and used His influence to keep that mean-spirited villain out of work for the rest of his days).

But even this was not enough. At the age of thirty, Jesus still felt empty. What it was He could not tell. And then His old friend, John the Baptist, re-entered the picture. Strolling one day, by the River Jordan, Jesus noticed a small crowd of people standing on the bank. As He drew nearer He saw a familiar figure at their head. Drawing still nearer, He saw that it was His old friend John, and that, one by one, He seemed to be washing the assembled company.

"John," cried Jesus, running up, "John the Baptist! My old friend—is that YOU?"

John, for it was he, turned slowly towards Jesus. "Yes it is I," affirmed the still young man, "but I am no longer your friend. I have no friend but the LORD. I am born-again, brother!"

Born again! Born again in the LORD! Perhaps, thought Jesus, that is what has been missing from my life! Pushing his way to the head of the line, he confronted John.

"I want to be born again. Right now!" He avowed thickly.

And bowing His head, Jesus allowed John to pour water on His head. And the heavens opened, and a hawk descended to hover over Jesus' head, and a great voice said: "This is my blessed Son—enter my world, please!"

A great sense of well-being swept over Jesus and He knew He had found the Answer. Whole now within and without, a prosperous businessman, a great athlete, pure in mind and body, the tall, blonde, muscular, energetic, considerate, experienced, forceful young man was finally ready for the mission chosen for Him from the beginning of time, four thousand and thirty-four years before.

Christ was ON HIS WAY!!

SEE AND BELIEVE!
MARVELOUS MAGICAL MIRACLES

The Amazing
Suicidal Swine!

The Miraculous Draught
of Fishes!

The Calming
of the Winds!

Internationally
World
Famous

Eternal
Secret
Mysteries
Revealed

JESUS H. CHRIST

Spectacular Effects!
Fabulous Feats

Sleight of Hand!
Supernatural Wonders!

👉 OLD TIME REVIVAL MEETING 👈
CRUSADE
AND TRAVELING
MEDICINE SHOW!

WATER INTO WINE!

This amusing, entertaining, and tasteful "experiment" is sure to make a "hit" at wedding feasts and other social functions! With a wave of your hand, you appear to transform ordinary tap water into wine!!!

The secret, of course, is our patented Aqua-Vino© waterpot (available in 2 and 3 firkin sizes).

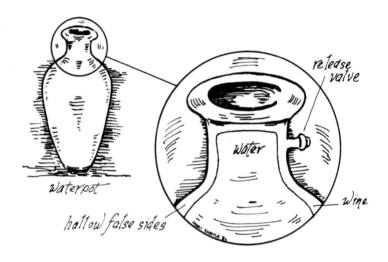

Instructions: Before performing this "Miracle," the "Magician" surreptitiously substitutes the Aqua-Vino© waterpot.

With a "Magical" wave of the hand, he presses the release valve (fig. B).

The wine (or grape juice) which is stored in the hidden bottle neck reservoir, will flow down the "false" or "hollow" sides of the bottle, creating the effect of transforming the water into wine!

N.B.: This "Wonder" is best accomplished after the guests have consumed rather a lot of wine. When they taste your "Magic" wine, they might actually maintain that it is better than what they tasted previously!

THE SECRET OF THE INCREDIBLE MULTIPLYING LOAVES AND FISHES

At a dinner party, or any social gathering around the "Festive Board," what entertainment could be more delightful than a combination of "conjuring" and "catering?"

The multitudes are certain to worship you when you produce, from a simple basket, a sufficiency of the "Staff of Life" and "Finny Denizens of the Deep" to feed all and sundry . . . with numerous comestibles *left over!*

Here is the long-kept secret of Jesus H. Christ's most popular effect!

This illusion is accomplished with the aid of an assistant, or "Apostle," who crouches beneath the surface of the "prepared" table and passes loaves and fishes up through the basket into the hands of the "Master."

If the effect is to be attempted in the out-of-doors, more elaborate advanced preparation, that is digging a hole in the mountain side of sufficient size to accommodate the Apostle and the victuals, will be necessary.

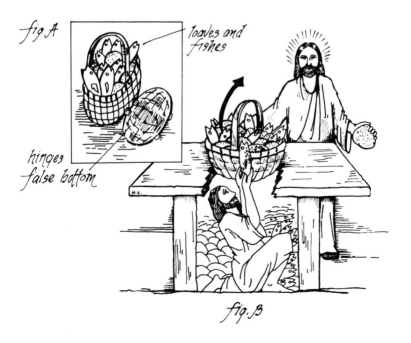

fig. A

loaves and fishes

hinges false bottom

fig. B

THE "DEATH-DEFYING" WALK ON WATER

Imagine the surprise of your Brethren and Disciples who are "out for a sail," when they suddenly see you approaching, and walking upon the surface of the water!

In the words of many a spectator, this illusion is "Just Divine!"

And here's how it's done:

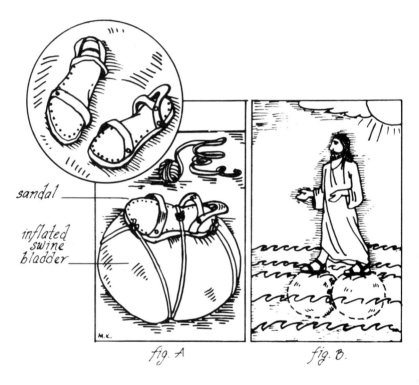

sandal

inflated
swine
bladder

fig. A

fig. B.

To the bottoms of an ordinary pair of sandals are affixed the inflated bladders of two Garadene Swine (fig. A).

N.B.: This effect requires much private practice! Rehearse in shallow pools before attempting it on the surface of the sea! A slow, stately walking style is necessary—but adds much to the beauty of the spectacle! (fig. B).

THE ELECTRIFYING "TRANSFIGURATION" ILLUSION

This "Show Stopper" is a multitude-pleasing effect which was only occasionally performed by Dr. Christ. Like most "spectacular" effects, it is, in reality, more easily accomplished than many "close-up" sleight-of-hand illusions, e.g. "Making the Blind to See"—in which "the hand" must be, indeed, "quicker than the eye."

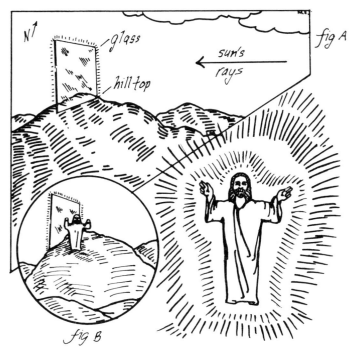

This illusion should be attempted only at sunrise, and performed atop a hill facing East. A highly polished, completely transparent pane of glass—we recommend the "Beatific Vision" or "Sun of God" models—should be previously erected on the hill top (fig. A).

The glass will be quite invisible to on-lookers, but the rays of the rising sun, striking it, will create an impression glorious to behold—and quite unforgettable! (fig. B).

TWO HEADED CAESAR

A "volunteer" from the multitude (actually a Disciple in disguise) asks the Illusionist a "trick" question. After deep thought, the Master replies that he will discover the answer by tossing a coin. The "volunteer," by pre-arrangement, hands him up a coin—and the multitudes are astonished to discover that the "Answer" is always "Caesar!"

How is this achieved? By means of the "Two Headed," or "Two Faced," coin pictured below!

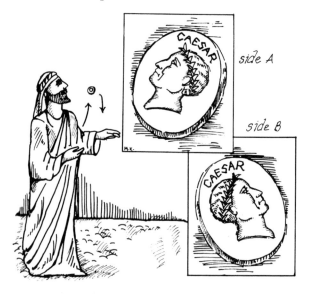

side A

side B

THE "LAZARUS EFFECT": THE AMAZING, THRILLING ILLUSION OF RESURRECTION FROM THE DEAD!
or
"THE OLD TWO-COFFIN TRICK"

In plain view of a great multitude, a three-day-old corpse is placed in a coffin. Trustworthy members of the multitude, such as publicans and tax collectors, are asked to inspect the coffin, to place it in a tomb, and to verify that the tomb has been "sealed" shut with a large rock.

"THE OLD TWO-COFFIN TRICK"

After several moments of intense suspense, while the Master "prays," he gives the command for the tomb to be unsealed, and the coffin to be brought back out.

When the coffin is, in turn, opened—Lazarus "comes forth!"

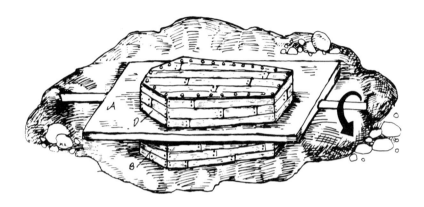

The ingenious secret to the "Lazarus Effect" lies in careful rehearsal, the correct apparatus, and proper preparation.

Inside the tomb is a platform (A) on which the coffin (B) will be placed. This platform is balanced on a pivot (C). Beneath the platform is another, identical coffin (D).

Once the tomb is sealed, the (very much alive) occupant of coffin (D), an associate and Disciple of the Master, simply shifts his weight, causing the platform to turn, coffin (B) to "disappear" beneath, and coffin (D), containing the living man, to be in position to be removed and opened by the unsuspecting and astonished members of the public.

There is reason to believe that Dr. Christ, that most accomplished Prestidigitator, may some day attempt the "Lazarus Effect" with Himself as the "subject"—in other words, "raise Himself" from "the dead."

Were He to attempt—and accomplish—this operation, there is little doubt it would be numbered among the Grandest Illusions of history!

"I am come that you might have life— and that you might have them more abundantly!"

BEFORE

AFTER

It's a Miracle!

Yes, as any of you regular watchers of the **695 Club** can testify, each week, right here on **this** stage, without any medical training **whatsoever**, we heal and cure and perform brain surgery and do orthodontic work in the name of the **Lord!** And when our nationwide audience sees, and believes, **it's a Miracle!**

His Mysterious Ways!

Yes, following the example of the **Master**, we perform prodigious feats of therapeutic and fiscal **prestidigitation**, for Christ's sake! The blind walk, the deaf are made to see, and cripples to hear, according to the **mystery** of **faith!** But why?

The Teaching Ministry

And so, following the Lord's **Divine Example**, we raise the dead and wither figs and so forth to **get their attention!** For it is then that we can impart the wonderful **message** of the Gospel, or **Good News!**

But Why?

We preachers of the gospel work these wonders not for their sake alone, as the **false magicians** of Chaldea do! Our ministry is not to **heal** only, but to **teach!** Yeah, the healing part is just to **get them into the tent**, as the saying is!

Stay Tuned!

Coming right up, is the most **exciting** and **entertaining** part of our whole Book! So, won't you give a very warm, very attentive Christian ear to our next Gospel, a little thing we like to call . . .

THE WIT AND WISDOM

OF JESUS CHRIST

EVEN the just-plain-*funniest* of Jesus' jokes always had a point to them ... a message, a lesson, a moral—call it what you will.

For instance, He was on tour in Galilee, curing cripples and lepers, when a one-eyed man came unto Him, to be healed.

Jesus politely asked the man to take his place in line, and to pay Judas, who at that time was Secretary of the Treasury.

But the one-eyed man cried out in a loud voice, saying, "Lord, I am poor. Neither have I money, nor scrip nor shoes, nor even a place whereon to lay my head!"

Now, Jesus always considered the doctor-patient relationship to be a sacred one, and maintained that the passing of silver was an essential part of the ritual. He saw that He had a chance to make a point here, and quickly summoned His disciples to gather 'round.

"Behold," He said, "this man cometh unto me with neither gold nor riches, nor any other offering, but only with faith." Then, turning to the one-eyed man, He asked of him, "My son, what wouldst thou have me do?"

"Lord," he replied, "I pray that thou wouldst make my one eye like unto the other."

Then Jesus smiled, and looked up to Heaven, and laid His hands upon the head of the one-eyed man.

And lo! he was totally blind.

As you can imagine, the disciples marvelled much at this, but Jesus said unto them, "What then didst thou expect? For verily, in this world, thou gettest whatsoever thou payest for."

A VOICE ON THE WILDERNESS

JESUS personally had a great love for the wilderness, and would sometimes wander off by Himself for forty days and forty nights of peace and quiet in the desert.

Many of His apostles were dedicated *fishermen*. Avid huntsmen as well, they often went together on expeditions into the Judean hills, after the fabled black sheep there.

But Jesus had no patience with conservation extremists, those 'eco-nut' types who opposed clear-cutting the Cedars of Lebanon, advocated catch quotas on the Sea of Galilee, lobbied to impose undue regulations on the Milk and Honey industry, or were agitating to ban the *Balm in Gilead*.

One time, when He was addressing a multitude, Jesus noticed that He was being constantly interrupted by a bunch of long-haired kooks, who called themselves "The Friends of the Locust."

Turning to them, Jesus pointed to a nearby meadow, full of blooming flowers, and shut them up for good with this witty quip:

"Behold the lilies of the field; for verily, I say unto you, that they causeth ninety percent of pollution."

YOU *CAN* TAKE IT WITH YOU

ONCE, a gang of wide-eyed Zealots, pushing a so-called 'reform' issue to extremes, invaded the Temple, and drove out all the money changers working there, calling it 'a den of thieves.'

Now, as Jesus never tired of reminding His followers, the Temple belonged to His family, and would some day be His. So many members of the Media immediately came unto Him, for a hastily convened Scribe's Conference—and they started giving Jesus a hard time about the tax-free status of business conducted in the Temple.

"I come not to destroy the law and the profits," Jesus assured them, "but to make sure they work together."

Then, departing from his prepared text, the Resourceful Redeemer ad libbed: "Verily, I say unto you, it is no harder for a rich man to enter the Kingdom of Heaven than for a needle to go through the eye of a camel."

WELL, WELL, WELL...

JOHN, who was the youngest and best-looking of all the Apostles, went on to write a popular, if un-authorized biography of the Master. He tells this one:

It seems one time Jesus was passing through a hick town, a real little one-ass place, down in Samaria.

Everybody knows better than to drink the water down in Samaria, but this day Jesus was drier than a withered fig, so He went on over to the local well, a place called Jacob's.

Now, water's pretty scarce in those parts, but here's this native woman, who looks about half Samaritan, one quarter Nubian and with a little Philistine thrown in, and she's hauling out that water by the bucketful!

Jesus asked her for a drink. But she said there wasn't hardly enough there for her! "What about your husband?" Jesus asks, cool as a Canaanite.

She says she doesn't have a husband.

"Damn right you don't," says Jesus. "You've probably got *five* of them!"

Well of course the funny thing is, she *did* have five of them! Her eyes about popped out of her head, and right away she gave Jesus a drink, and poured the rest of that water back into the well.

It's another cute story, but it has a point to it, too. There's a big difference between using the well fairly, and living off welfare.

GOOD NEIGHBORS

SPEAKING of Samaritans, Jesus likes to tell a little story about one of them, to show that a man could be moral and upright and do the right thing, no matter what his color or where he came from.

There was this traveling salesman, on his way from Jerusalem to Jericho. And wouldn't you know it, he got mugged. They took his money, and his clothes, and beat the daylights out of him, and left him laying there about half dead.

Well, first, along comes a clergyman, maybe a priest or something, you know the type. He sees the fellow lying there, and walks right on by.

Next, along comes a lawyer, who's probably so busy thinking about criminals' rights, he walks by too or maybe he just didn't want to get involved.

Then who should come by, but a Samaritan. He took a look at that man lying there in the ditch, all naked and beat up, and by God, even if he was just a Samaritan, he knew what to do.

He lit out after that gang of thieves, and he tracked them down. And when he caught up with them—they were Samaritans too, by the way—he didn't waste any time asking questions.

One by one, he killed them. Slow, so they'd have time to think about it.

Which just goes to show you that Samaritans are hardest on their own.

ON SPANKING

"LET the little children suffer, who come unto me."

ON CHURCH AND STATE

"WHAT God has joined together, let no man put asunder."

ON A SOUND ENERGY POLICY

JESUS didn't go in for 'off color' stories, unless they made a good point. Here's a 'spicey one' he came up with at the Last Smoker.

It seems there were ten virgins, waiting for this bridegroom to come home. Now, five of them were wise virgins, who used domestic oil on their lamps, but the other five were foolish, and used imported oil.

Now because of some ruckus overseas, there wasn't any oil for the foolish virgins to use, and they asked the wise virgins if they could borrow some.

"Go get it from your Arab friends," said the wise virgins.

So when the bridegroom got home, the foolish virgins were sitting around in the dark.

And in the morning, there were five girls who were still foolish, but no longer virgins—and five virgins who were none the wiser!

ON THE AFTERLIFE

JESUS used to like to tell a story about a poor leper, named Lazarus, and a rich man, named Dives. Well, they both die, and go to heaven, and there's St. Peter waiting for them at the Pearly Gates.

Peter says, "Before I let either of you inside, tell me about yourselves."

So Lazarus describes how he caught leprosy by hanging around with lepers, and how he lived on handouts all his life.

Then Dives describes how much money he had, and his investment portfolio, and so forth, and then he slips Peter a little something as a token of his esteem.

"I'm sorry," Peter says to Lazarus, "but down you go!" He pulls a lever, and a trap door opens, and bye-bye Lazarus!

"Come on in," he says to Dives. And Dives is just about to go in, when he has a thought. "Hold on a minute, Peter," he says. "Because I'm not going in if you have Roosevelt in there!"

Peter slaps him on the back, and says, "Don't be silly. Roosevelt's downstairs, where he belongs."

Well, Dives goes through the gates, and starts walking around, and the first thing he sees is this man in a wheel chair, smoking a cigaret in a long holder, with a Scottie dog in his lap!

Dives turns to St. Peter, and says "I thought you said Roosevelt was downstairs!"

"Don't worry," says Peter. That's not Roosevelt, that's God! He just *thinks* he's Roosevelt!

AN AFTER-DINNER SPEECH IN THE MOUNTAINS

ONE time, Jesus saw that there was a great multitude gathered together, and that the multitude was mostly moral, and so He stood up on a mountain side, and addressed them. This is what He said, pretty much *verbatim*:

Blessed are the truly needy: for they shall have a safety net.

Blessed are they that own much: for they shall be sheltered.

Blessed are the arms bearers: for they shall inherit the earth.

Blessed are they that do thunder and curse on the right, such as us: for they shall get elected.

Blessed are the powerful: for they shall seize power.

Blessed are the prudes at heart: for they shall see sex everywhere.

Blessed are the peace officers: for they shall be called to testify with immunity.

Blessed are they who are appointed unto high positions: for theirs is a piece of the action.

Blessed are you, when the scribes of the press which is liberal revile you, and ridicule you, and publish all manner of evil against you, just because it happeneth to be true: for Heaven's sake.

Rejoice, and be exceeding glad, for great is your reward, and so persecuted were the makers of profits before you.

You have heard of the SALT of the earth. But if the SALT should commence to talk, what then of the cellar? Verily, he looseth his contracts, and is cast out of work, with an huge inventory.

You are to the Right of the world. A City that is set upon a Hill cannot be hid. It crieth out, therefore, for an adequate defense system.

So if thy right wing offend thee, look to it, and ask thyself, wherein have I sinned? But if thy left wing offend thee, cut it off, and cast it from thee.

You have heard it said, An eye for an eye, and a tooth for a tooth.

But I say unto you that he who first blindeth, and rendereth toothless the other guy hath little to fear from him.

The Lord's School Prayer

Federally Inspected, Cleared, Approved
Recommended and Compulsory for use in all Schools,
both Public and Private

Our Father which art in
   Heaven, Hello and
      what's Your Name?
By thinking none, we will be dumb
In class, as they are in Heaven.
Give us this day our daily bread,
   but no lunch,
And LORD, give us no school buses
As we will give no school buses
   to them that are against us.
And teach us nothing but Creation,
But deliver us from evolution,
For Thine is the Republic,
And the power of Old Glory,
For ever and ever.
Amen.

Love's Thorny Crown

THE GOSPEL ACCORDING TO
ROSEMARY

Another 'Divine' Romance©
by the authoress of

THE PASSION IN THE GARDEN
& SIN'S FIERY TORMENT

I

Gethsemane. I was only a girl still, although already blooming with the promise of a woman's lushness, when I first
heard the name of the place spoken. Gethsemane! Even then,
my slender frame trembled at the sound of the word, with its
deep overtones of night, torch light, and flashing swords,
while my cheeks warmed and reddened to its sweet angelic
harmonies of tears, and pain, and Love Everlasting.

Little did I think then, that one dark and dangerous night,
I would be *there*, with *Him*, in Gethsemane. . .

"Mary! Mary Magdalene! You come down here, girl, and
get to work!" My reveries were shattered by this harsh but
shrill voice. I had been gazing dreamily out the window, at
the busy streets and quiet hills of my native city, Jerusalem.
It was a beautiful April morning, in the year 33 A.D.

The cruel but well-disciplined armies of Imperial Rome
had occupied Judea, my homeland, while conquering most
of the known world, and our so-called King Herod was only
the sensuous degenerate pawn of the intelligent but indeci-
sive Governor Pontius Pilate, who took his orders directly
from the ancient Roman Emperor, Tiberius.

Some of our leaders, called Pharisees, counseled collabo-
ration and patience beneath the yoke of oppression, while
others, the Zealots, advocated a violent, revolutionary over-
throw of the system. It was the age-old conflict of cool and
thoughtful brain versus hot and passionate heart, I reflected
with a pensive shrug, as I gave my long and luxuriant raven-
black hair a final brush stroke and turned from daydreaming
at the casement to do my employer's bidding.

I had been born to haughty and aristocratic parents in
Galilee, in Magdela, the town which yet bears our ancient
family name. But all that we possessed, including the lives
of my dear parents, had been lost in the bloody rebellion of
the two Rabbis Judah and Mattathias, who ten years before
had endeavored to remove from above the Temple gate the
Roman eagle which they regarded as a symbol of idolatry.
Both they and their suspected sympathizers were slaughtered.

Thus, at a tender age, I had to make my way alone in the
world, and found employment in a capacity which I considered beneath my proud station, yet not altogether unworthy
(for it is a saying among my people that "A young woman

must eat"). It was an occupation my magnificent light-brown long hair made me ideally suited for. I was a foot annointer.

Madam Judith, the ribald but kind-hearted old woman who served as my landlady and employer, had prepared for me the customary alabaster box of costly spikenard ointment, and now gave me directions to the house where the annointing was to be given.

It was in Bethany, a suburb situated a mile and a half away, outside the walls of Jerusalem, she said. So. An out-of-town job. "At the home," she added, "of Simon the Leper".

"You know I don't do lepers," I shouted, indignantly.

II

With Madam Judith's chuckling assurance that it was not the leper's feet I was to annoint, nor the doubtless equally disgusting extremities of another of the invited guests, Lazarus, who had been dead, I set out down the Jericho highway, toward Bethany.

I was delighted to discover that the house was a charming edifice, of pre-Roman design, and in much better preserved condition than its owner, Simon. He greeted me at the back door, and kindly offered me his hand (which I was later able to dispose of behind a potted palm, when no one was looking).

Tonight's foot-annointing was to be a surprise for the guest of honor at supper, and I was told to remain hidden in the kitchen, until I was summoned.

Through the curtains which served as a door to the dining room, I was able to observe the festivities in progress.

Lazarus, the recently deceased, was at the table, but no one sat near him, nor down wind of him. Martha, his ugly sister, bustled about, shining the silverware, pouring wine and serving meat, and was generally ignored, while his pretty sister (whose name, like mine, was Mary,) sat gazing worshipfully into the eyes of whomever was speaking, and was therefore the object of much admiration and attention.

The room was crowded with neighbors who had dropped by to pay their respects at Lazarus' funeral breakfast, and stayed over for the resurrection supper, yet all eyes—and mine, too, I confess—were focused on a handsome, blonde, bearded young stranger at the head of the table.

As I stared at Him from my hiding place, I felt an indescribable thrill course through my voluptuous and firm-breasted body, as if those old-familiar seven devils were once more loosed in my heart. I dared to hope that it was He whose sensitive feet I would soon be smearing with costly spikenard, and drying with my auburn tresses.

Lest I should cry out in this whirlwind of ecstasy, I bit my full, trembling lower lip, and averted my gaze to the kitchen window. Beyond, in the twilight, stood the Mount of Olives, upon whose sunset enpurpled slopes lay, I realized with a gasp, *Gethsemane.*

III

Nervously, feverishly, I awaited my cue to enter the room. Simon, the host, had said he would cast an eye in my direction when it was time. He did so now, and it narrowly missed me, striking the door post.

To the astonished but delighted applause of the guests, I made my entrance, dancing and twirling, swirling seductively, tauntingly, teasingly, bending and swaying, for I was determined that this would be the performance of a life time!

I stood before the tall, handsome guest of honor, and gazed deep into his flashing yet sensitive blue eyes. I could feel the seven devils in my heart dancing to a pagan rhythm, as I slowly removed the alabaster box from the folds of my gossamer skirts. I paused, and a hush descended as I extended, and held still, the sealed container before His face. Then, with a sudden gesture of surrender, I broke the box.

First, I allowed a few slow drops of the costly ointment to fall upon his head, and to mingle there with His silky hair, which was nearly as long, and quite as golden, as my own. He smiled at me, such a knowing, loving, gentle smile as I had never before beheld, and His smile seemed to somehow still the rampaging of the seven devils in my heart.

Slowly, our eyes still locked with tender intensity, I crouched, then knelt, before Him. Now my glance fell to His feet, long, and sensitive, and naked, and of a hue every bit as alabaster as my own precious ointment box.

I turned my wrist, and poured. The sweet-smelling, creamy spikenard emerged, first in a few translucent drops, then with a sudden gushing, until His feet glistened wetly.

He spoke not a word, as I lifted my face to look into His

once more. I raised my hand to the ribbon which bound my tresses, and, with a gentle tug, unleashed and loosed my hair, which tumbled down in copper-red cascades of glory.

Now I bowed low once more, and, tossing my head slowly, rhythmically, from side to side, suffered my curls to dry His annointed feet.

Suddenly, harshly, the electric silence was broken by a deep rasping cry of protest.

"What a waste!" barked his voice from above, and I glanced up, startled, into the black-bearded, hawk-like and swarthy visage of a burning-eyed Zealot. Judas Iscariot!

IV

The Iscariot family had lived next door to us, in the old days, in Galilee. Because old Simon Iscariot was a Temple money-changer, society looked down on them as *nouveau-riche*, but they were very *riche* indeed. Their home had been one of the most splendid mansions near my father's house.

As a child, I had not been allowed to play with little Judas, but nevertheless we had been friends, and more than friends, sharing the excitement only secret and forbidden meetings have. On moonlit nights, on the banks of the flowing Jordan, he would whisper to me of his hate for the foreign idolaters, and of his dreams of a Palestinian homeland—and together we would explore, with the eager hands and clumsy mouths of innocence, the small dark places in the honeycomb of first love.

I thought surely Judas had died ten years ago in the massacre, or at least fled into Egypt. And now—to see him again—like this—as I knelt before another, my hair dripping with ointment—to see his black eyes blazing with jealousy—was almost more than I could bear. I gasped.

He turned to the handsome stranger, whom he called (and I, too, would learn to call) "Master." "Master," he growled, "why was not this ointment sold for three hundred pence, and given to the poor?"

The same old Judas, I thought, fondly, remembering that even as a boy he carried everywhere his little bag of money, and would never part with a sheckle for a tasty treat, a date or fig, because he was "Saving up to buy a sword for the revolution." Even then I loved him for his bravery and self-discipline, and now, as I heard the Master answer him, my foolish heart was torn between my old love for this fierce and frugal Zealot, and my new love for this gentle man of peace from Nazareth.

The Master said to Judas, "Why are you bothering her? Let her alone. There have always been poor people, and there will always be poor people, and that's life. But this was something *special*." He put his hands on my shoulders, and said to me, very softly, but loud enough for the others to hear, "In times to come, when people speak of me—and they *will*—I want them to remember what you did for me tonight."

My heart melted like snow in the spring sun, as I heard these words spoken by the Master, yet I confess I was thrilled and flattered too by the passionate reply of Judas, my childhood sweetheart.

"Get yourself another bag man, Nazarite!" he snarled, as he tore a purse of coins from his belt and flung it on the table, and stormed out the door, before slamming it behind him.

I know now that Judas went directly into Jerusalem to the high priests, to betray the Master. I suppose Hell hath no fury like a Zealot scorned, either.

V

The next morning was a Sunday. In two days I knew, Passover (Pesach) would begin, which is a week-long seven days of High Holy Days commemorating the deliverance of the children of Israel (Jacob) from the Angel of Death during the time of the Egyptian captivity.

Normally, Passover was a bonanza for we in the profession, because many wealthy tourists came to Jerusalem to celebrate with wine, foot annointings and song, and there was big money to be made.

But, next morning, as I stood once more at my former window, brushing my chestnut colored curls in the sunlight, I beheld a wonderful sight in the street below. A crowd like a procession was singing and shouting and breaking the branches off the palm trees that lined the avenue, and littering the roadway with them.

I recognized Peter, the big fisherman, and John, the fair slender and delicate youth, and James Greater and James the

Lesser, and others I had met at the party in Bethany.

Then I saw . . . Him! He was clothed all in white raiment, with a cloak of seamless crimson thrown casually over His shoulders, with hand-tooled leather sandals and matching accessories. He rode upon a milk-white ass, the most beautiful ass I had ever beheld, and acknowledged the plaudits of the multitude with truly regal humility. I gasped.

Though I could scarcely tear my gaze from Him, in vain did I scour the crowd of followers and spectators for a glimpse of the moody and tempestuous Judas.

In a flash, as if I had been knocked from a horse on the road to Damascus, I made my decision. I dashed down the stairs, and, despite the puzzled and angry protestations of my employer, ran out into the street and joined the parade. Call it fate, I reflected, or Divine Providence . . . I was His, eternally. Or call it love.

And little did I know that at that very moment, love was working a darker miracle elsewhere, as Judas, my impetuous childhood sweetheart, driven half mad by that old green-eyed demon, Jealousy, was accepting thirty pieces of silver from the evil Caiaphas, for the promise of treason.

VI

So I became a disciple, accepted openly by such as Peter, that great cuddly teddy bear of an apostle, quick to tears and quicker to loud, hearty laughter—and accepted grudgingly by others, such as the sulking and sensitive young John, who seemed to resent my special closeness with the Master.

For three whole, wonderful days I watched as He preached to enthusiastic audiences from the steps of the Temple. And when they would interrupt His parables with wild, enthusiastic cheers and applause, it thrilled me to the very quick to know that in the evening I alone of all that multitude would be alone with Him, gently and tenderly annointing His beloved feet, and drying them with my soft ebony ringlets.

The second night, I remember, oh! so clearly! I knelt before Him, exhausted but exhilarated after the tenderest, wildest, and most meaningful annointing of my life.

And then, for the first time since that evening in Bethany, the Master spoke to me. I'll never forget His words, as He said, in a whisper tinged with a sort of divine sadness, "What is your name, woman?"

"Mary," I replied.

"Mary?" he gasped. And then he uttered, with a far away look in his soft yet fiery eyes, "That was my mother's name!"

VII

At sunset on Thursday, the Passover Festival exploded. In the dusty cobbled streets of old Jerusalem, and along its broad and palm-lined avenues, the joyous Hebrews, their ceremonial garb a riot of colors, danced the traditional wild *horas*, and sang lustily the old songs celebrating the mercy of Yahweh, who had caused the first-born man children of Egypt to die in their cradles in unspeakable agony.

In a room above, the Master held the *Seder*, a formal feast featuring *matzoh* (unleavened bread), bitter herbs, and wine. All twelve of His close friends, or "Apostles," as He called them, were gathered together. Even Judas Iscariot was there. We women disciples remained in a room below, and when Judas passed the door on his way to the room upstairs, I turned my head, for I dared not meet his accusing eyes.

All the world knows what transpired in the Upper Room that night, and others, who's story-telling gifts far exceed mine, have described the conversation, the blessing of the bread and wine, the Master's firm but gentle rebuke to Judas, and Iscariot's headlong, guilty dash from the house.

I, being but a woman, was not present, and learned all only later, in the magnificent if somewhat contradictory versions of Matthew, Mark, Luke, and John, all of whom were eye witnesses, but all of whom, if you ask me, had over-indulged in the ceremonial wine.

Soon enough, we women folk heard the hymn being sung in the room above, and then the tramp of manly feet upon the stair, as the Master and his Apostles descended.

I asked Mary, the beautiful sister of Lazarus, who had been with the Master longer than I—(why, I wondered, did He favor women with my name?)—whither they might be bound.

"Over the brook Cedron," she replied, "for they oft times resort thither, to the Mount of Olives, where there is a garden called Gethsemane."

Gethsemane! The word pierced me, like a whirlwind-driven

wave of flame! And I knew I must follow, come what may!

Of course, it was our part, as women, to stay behind and clear the table, but since Lazarus' other sister, Martha, who absolutely *loved* washing up, was among us, I felt no twinge of guilt as I wrapped a shawl around my pale ash-blonde head, and hurried away after them, to Gethsemane.

VIII

In the darkness I climbed the slope, through the olive-scented night breezes. Because there was no moon, I feared to lose my way, and was startled with terror when I nearly stumbled over a body lying in the shadows. I gasped, and with difficulty contained a cry of fear.

With relief, my eyes made out in the darkness the sleeping face of one of the sons of Zebedee. But my relief turned to sudden anger, as I realized that this man, who had doubtless been posted sentry to guard the Master, was asleep on duty! Roughly I kicked his recumbent form, until he shuddered, and sat upright. "If you can't hold your wine," I whispered harshly, "stay out of the Seder! Now, keep your eyes open! There's something wrong here. I can feel it in my bones. It's quiet. Too quiet."

Resentful yet grateful, the sentry staggered to his feet, and resumed scanning the darkness, as I left him there.

I brushed aside olive branches, and came upon a clearing. Suddenly, miraculously, the moon peeped out from a wrack of clouds, sending a single bright beam down to illuminate Him—the Master! He was kneeling, His classically perfect profile to the heavens, and the moonlight made a halo of His fine, shoulder-length golden hair.

Never before, not even in our most intimate moments together, had I beheld Him wearing so intense, so passionate, and yet so vulnerable a facial expression. Once more, a surging flood of blazing adoration raced through my veins, and it was all I could do to restrain myself from rushing out to him and annointing those adorable feet once more...

But then, from the corner of my tear-dimmed eye, I caught a glimmer, a spark, a flash of light, as of a torch approaching up the hillside through the trees! It was on the slope opposite that guarded by the sentry I had awakened! Where were the other apostles? Wildly, feverishly, I glanced about.

There! Not a stone's throw away, they were gathered, and all, even Peter, stretched upon the ground, asleep!

Headlong, I ran among the wine-besotted sleepers, slapping, pinching, kicking. As each in turn blinked awake, startled, I put a finger to his lips, mutely commanding silence, and pointed toward the approaching army of torch bearers. In stealthy silence, each newly-wakened Apostle grasped the situation, and quietly drew his blade.

Breathlessly we watched, as into the clearing where the Master knelt came—Judas! For a long moment he stood, staring intensely upon his beloved enemy, his hated friend. Then, he glanced quickly and conspiratorially over his shoulder at the troops behind him, strode quickly across the clearing, bent, and kissed the Master upon the lips.

Suddenly I remembered (and the resurrected seven devils danced once more in my racing heart) those first-love kisses of his and mine, on the banks of the Jordan, so long ago.

Now, into the clearing, bearing torches, and swords, and staves, crashed a band of men from the chief priests and Pharisees.

Judas, his eyes dim with passion, stepped away from the Master, who Himself turned to face the armed men. "Whom seek you," He enquired, calmly, stalling for time.

They answered Him, "Jesus of Nazareth."

"I am He," replied the Master, and this must have been the agreed-upon signal, for with a brave cry the Apostles charged out of their hiding place, and attacked.

"The ears!" shouted Peter, "Go for the ears," and he himself, with a swift thrust, sliced the aural appendage off the startled head of the high priest's servant.

Now this way, now that, the battle raged in the flickering shadows of that torch-lit garden. The calm darkness of the spring night was rent with the clash of blade upon blade, stave upon stave, and with the fearful howls of the Pharisees' officers, as their ears fell like leaves in an autumn hurricane.

Yet the Apostles, brave and daring swordsmen as they were, were fearfully out-numbered, and forced to fall back before the Roman-army trained forces, until one hulking brute, the hated high priest Caiaphas himself, broke through the line and seized the Master, his sword drawn!

As in a dream, everyone froze, swords and staves in mid thrust, watching Caiaphas, who held the Master's arm behind

His back with his left hand, while his right pressed the deadly blade of Roman steel against the pale white column of the Master's throat.

I shall never know why I turned at that moment to look at Judas. Perhaps I was thinking, even then, that however much I adored the Master for His gentleness, I dared to wish He possessed some of the Iscariot strength, anger, and fierceness.

On the black-bearded, hawk-like handsome face of my old love, the Zealot, the flickering torch light performed a passion play of emotions.

True, the Master had stolen away the heart of His own true love, me, and against this Judas' proud heart cried out for vengeance. And yet, that was a *Roman* sword, at the throat of a fellow Israelite...

Quicker than the beat of a passionate heart, Judas lept forward, in his hand a blade forged true in Judah, on his lips the old battle cry, "For Zion!"

The startled Caiaphas turned, releasing the Master, and lashed out at his attacker. Judas' aim was true—his naked blade pierced the chest of the evil high priest—yet with the desperate dying strength of the damned, Caiaphas, too, thrust home, and Judas fell, his blood gushing forth like a river of scarlet honor.

Heedless of danger, I ran to him, from my hiding place, flung myself down beside him, and cradled his head in my lap. I bent to kiss, one last time, those brave familiar lips, and heard him whisper, faintly, "The feet. Mary. The feet."

More completely defeated than they might have been by twelve legions of angels, the High Priest's officers and troops withdrew, and faded into the night.

The Master stood beside us a while, but could say nothing, for there was nothing He could say. Together with his Apostles, He, too, wandered away down the mountain side, in the silence of bitter-sweet triumph.

And all that long night, I washed the feet of Judas with his own heart's blood, and dried them with my hair, until day broke over the Judean hills, and Joseph of Aramethea, an old friend, came and took away his body, to prepare it for burial. It had already, I explained to Joseph, been annointed.

And now the second Sabbath of Passover is over, and it is Sunday morning, before dawn. And I am standing in the Garden, beside the tomb of Judas. And I am waiting.

"Hi there."

I *want you to walk with me now in the foot-*
steps of a truly great man, someone who's
done wonders for Christianity through the
ages. His name? Paul the Apostle.

"Almost single-handed Paul set the rec-
ord straight on just what that enigmatic charac-
ter Jesus had really *meant.*

"How did he do this? Well, he wrote letters.
These letters were called Epistles. *But did Paul*
just get an idea for an Epistle and sit down and
write it? Of course not.

"Many early Christians were confused about
their new religion. They needed help and guid-
ance to avoid the bottomless pit of eternal dam-
nation. So they wrote to Paul. And, workaholic
though he was, Paul always found time to write
back, from Rome or Jerusalem or wherever his
busy schedule took him.

"He was a friendly folksy sort of person was
Paul, a big bear of a fellow who liked people to
call him by his nickname "Appy"—short for 'The
Apostle.'

"Those early Christian questions and his an-
swers are as fresh and relevant today as they
were close on two thousand years ago.

"Here are some choice epistles from Appy's
mail-bag:"

DEAR APPY

DEAR APPY, I think I may be possessed. Often, when I am praying to my Savior OH JESUS, OH YES, O WHAT A FRIEND I HAVE IN ME, MORE TO THE LEFT OH GEE GOLLY WHILLIKERS THAT IS SO FINE O HONEY CHILD SO FINE SO FINE OH GOD OH GOD OH GOD OH GOOOOOOODD!!! YEEEEEAA-AAAOOOOOWWWWW! my mind goes completely blank for several moments. I am a widow and live on my own, so it's hard for me to tell if I am possessed but often after my prayers, my friends look at me funny. What do you think?
—POSSIBLY POSSESSED, CORINTH

PAUL, Specialist in Eternal Medicine, Licensed Layer-on of Hands:
TO POSSIBLY, Greetings: One think we knoweth for sure, O widow, that when thou prayeth, thou prayeth hard! Of thou truly may it be said—thou cameth to pray!

Naught in thy epistle leadeth me to think thou art possessed; only that thou overdoest it somewhat in the devotion department. Yet it is hard to judge since thou statest not thy age and weight. Thy weight bears on the matter since an unclean spirit dwelling within thee would add quite a load. If, howsoever, thou art a nice trim couple of bushels, and not too long in the tooth thou art probably as clean as a whistle.

Luckily I shall be in Corinth in a couple of weeks hence and shall come unto you; whereat the laying on of hands will tell us much. I shall bring also Timotheus, whose mystical massage has driven demons from many souls. Remember us in your prayers.

DEAR APPY, We are a small church in Phillipi and we are having trouble with our members. There aren't too many widows out in these parts so our members are always acting up. What can we do?
—CONCERNED EARLY CHRISTIAN, PHILLIPI

PAUL the Apostle, by the grace of God, Girder of loins, Safety Monitor of Souls:
TO EARLY, Greetings: I say unto you that be it never so hard, you must keep down the members of your church. For if those members rise up against you all shall then be lost. Try giving each guy a good-sized hammer.

DEAR APPY, I am a rich widow of saintly aspect. I have a grown son. He is an excellent student and has never needed scourging

to make him read his scriptures. Recently, though, he has begun acting real weird. He claims Jesus said we must sell all we have and give it to the poor. Where's the sense in that?
—WEALTHY AND WORRIED, TYRE

PAUL, Comptroller of the Lord, Tough Nut in the negotiations of Life:
TO WORRIED, Greetings: Let me say unto you something. It was not given to me to know Jesus personally, but I am acquainted with many who did. Jesus was an busy man; He was on the run always. Oftentimes He spake off the cuff. It was a mighty task to keep up with Him, and an even mightier one to keep proper records. Addeth thou to this that around Him were many misbegoten souls with their own axes to grind and thou hast a fine old mess. Wherefore it is not given to us alway to know exactly what things Jesus spake, nor what was in His mind. We must worketh it out for ourselves. So I say unto you, asketh thyself three questions:
1. Wherefore are the poor poor?
2. Wherewith will they spend the money?
3. Dost thou know why?
My guess, O widow, is that thou wilt answer in this wise:
1. Because they are lazy.
2. Drink and fornicate.
3. Nay.
Thus, if thou sellest all thou hast and giveth it to the poor, thou shalt lead them into sloth and drunkness and fornication whence they shall be damned and thou alongst with them. Was this what Jesus had in mind for thee? Nay, for sure. What seemeth much more likely is that He said: "Sell all thou hast and giveth it to Paul."

EPISTLE TO THE
EPHESIAN

DEAR APPY, My husband lives up a pole. He says it's the only way to get into heaven and that I'm damned. He won't let me sit with him, though, because his platform's too small. I'm supposed to get my own pole. All the same he expects me to bring him his bread and water every week. Appy, I'm tired of shinnying up that pole. I'm splinters all over. Am I damned? Should I get my own pole? Who'll bring *my* bread and water? What's the story?
—S. STYLITES (MRS.), EPHESUS

PAUL, by God's grace, Custodian of all his churches, Issuing Officer of His Summonses:
TO MRS. S., Greetings: Thy husband is a saint. Of course he's right to liveth up a pole, for lo, this bringeth him nearer to God, and is that not his duty as a man? *Thy* duty is to bring him his bread and water and give thanks unto the Lord thy God for every one of those splinters! Christ was a carpenter—did He mind splinters? But eschew thou thine own pole, for it is forbidden unto women to live up poles. I cannot say why, but it is. Art thou damned? Who knows? The rule of thumb is: wives are damned, widows aren't. Buckle to, serve thy husband, and no more of these whining epistles.

EPISTLE TO THE
THESSALONIANS

DEAR APPY, I am a teenage girl, and what I would like to know is, what is "fornication"? You keep mentioning it in your epistles and it sounds neat. Can I get some? My mother says no, but my friends say it's all over the place. What's it look like?

—HOPEFUL TEEN,
THESSALONIKA

PAUL, Strong Cleanser of Ingrained Filth, Catcher-Just-In-Time of Teenage Souls:

TO HOPEFUL, Greetings: FLEE FORNICATION!!! It is an horned monster that creepeth in the slime beneath the belly of the snake! Its hot sticky tongue inciteth to sin; its poisoned tail stingeth to perdition! And if thou dalliest with fornication, not only shalt thou be damned, thou shalt also get Pregnant with child! And thinkest not that thou canst get rid of it or fiddle around with some dohickey to prevent it in the first place, for these are greater sins even than fornication! So I say unto you O teens of Greece, keep thy mitts off one another! Go jump in the wine-dark sea and COOL OFF!

EPISTLE TO THE
ROMANS

DEAR APPY, We're a bunch of saints here in Rome and we have a question. In your last epistle —which was really great by the way—you said we should divide everything up "each according to his need." What we want to know is—does this mean share and share alike or does everyone get anything he says he needs? Like, what happens if some big saint comes up to you and says "I need your house"?

—THE BOYS, ROME

PAUL, Just Disposer of the Rules, First among Arbiters, Umpire of the Angels:

TONY, ANGIE, MOOK, AND THE MOB, Greetings: I say unto you, this is a toughie. Primo di primo, however, it doth NOT mean share and share alike. We all know where *that* leadeth. But lo, what it doth mean, is that the LORD in His wisdom did not build all saints the same. Taketh thou my assistant, and the guard of my body, Timotheus. He is a big solid saint. He *needeth* more than a smaller saint. He needeth more food, bigger sandals, a bigger cushion whereon to kneel. But that he may attain these things, doth he go around punching people out? Nay. I say unto you the key herewith is Giveth and Taketh. The smaller saints giveth, the bigger saints taketh. And if the smaller saints taketh what they need not, the bigger saints may taketh it back. But maketh thou not a lot of rules, for regulation is an abomination in the eyes of the LORD. Besides which it only giveth work to the lawyers, if thou catcheth my drift.

EPISTLE TO A
(SMALL) COLOSSIAN

DEAR APPY, My kid brother Hymeneus says Jesus has only one Nature. I say he has two. Who's right?

—ALEXANDER (AGED 6),
RHODES

PAUL, Forger of the Truth, Crossing Guard of the Narrow Way:

TO ALEXANDER, aged 6, Hi: Your kid brother is an heretic. Report him to the nearest saint.

EPISTLE TO
(CLASSIFIED)

DEAR APPY, (CLASSIFIED)

—(CLASSIFIED, somewhere in the
Mediterranean)

PAUL, First Agent of the Lord, Unhampered Operative of His Will:

TO (CLASSIFIED) who knows where he is, Greetings: Have no qualms, my son. Dost thou not show love unto thy enemy by giving him an express ticket to the afterlife? Get thou on with it. Waste the sucker. Eat this epistle if you're caught.

DEAR APPY, We live out here in Galatia. We know it's a long way from civilization but it sounds like a snappy name for a church. How can we start one?
> **—GUNG-HO GALATIANS,**
> **GALATIA**

PAUL, Earliest of Christians, Franchiser-in-Chief of the One True Faith:

TO A GUNG-HO GANG OF GALATIANS, Greetings: Thou betst it's a snappy name! I liketh it already. And heed not those who say "O foolish Galatians!"; for even out in the boonies there is no swifter way to store up riches for the LORD than the founding of a church. Canst thou take sweetmeat from a new new-born babe? This is easier. Consider thy tax breaks alone; on thy investment, on thy depreciation, on thy deficit financing, on all of these thou gettest a fat break. And shouldst thou build more than a church—let it be an hospital or an college or an gaming arena—thou gettest the same break for each one! Yea though thou build but the tenth part of each, still thou gettest the breaks. Nor is thy income subject to tax; nor that of the widow who giveth. Verily I say unto ye, Uncle Caesar practically payeth *ye* to found a church! Nor is this all, O wise Galatians, for ye may purchase all manner of goods, as chariots, books, casks of wine, instruments of music—so long as ye say they are needful for the business of thy church; and on these thou gettest yet another break!

Which is just; for are not such goods the Lord's? And art thou not simply their steward until He shall come again?

And yet I would caution thee in one wise: when ye build the church in Galatia, raise ye it up on a sandy plot. Heed not those who would counsel ye to build it on rock, for they have zero idea what it costeth to dig foundations therein. (Getteth me not wrong —I love Peter. Yet remember that in the Roman tongue his name signifieth 'rock' and ofttimes he thinketh like one).

Would ye know more, O Galatians? Then send for my fact-packed parchment "Reap Now, Sow Later"; and if ye taketh the plunge, I will send unto ye Timotheus, that he may aid in the raising of funds.

DEAR APPY, Are you a Jew or a Christian? We read everything you wrote about circumcision and that, but we just can't work it out. Fill us in.
> **—CONFUSED JEWS,**
> **CAESEREA**

PAUL, Jew, Gentile, Man of the Known World:

TO CONFUSED JEWS, Shalom and Ave: I am both. Lo, I am a son of Abraham, and a son of whoever started the Gentiles. I am circumcised and yet uncircumcised. Dost thou think then that I have two members? Nay—I am as other men. Yet only the tip is circumcised, while the rest is unso. Wherefore I am more a Christian than a Jew, but how *much* more, the Lord God hath forbidden me to say.

SECOND EPISTLE TO THE
EPHESIAN

DEAR APPY, While I was climbing up the pole to bring him his bread and water he fell off. I'm sure he was having one of his fits, but he says I jogged the pole and I'm damned. Am I? I said I was sorry and carried him back up, but he won't undamn me.
—S. STYLITES (MRS.),
EPHESUS

PAUL, Judge and Jury of the Chosen, Close Personal Friend of the Friends of Jesus:
TO MRS. S., Greetings: He's right. Thou art damned.

SECOND EPISTLE TO THE
THESSALONIANS

DEAR APPY, I am a young widow. When my atheistic, pleasure-seeking husband drowned recently in a feta barrel, I turned to the Church. The saints were great. They taught me to pray, to hope again, to laugh at my husband's death. But my son? Forget it! His father enrolled him in this experimental humanist school, and he refuses to leave. He says they're opening up his mind, but the other day I found him trying on my weeds! **—DESPERATE,**
THESSALONIKA

PAUL, by the grace of God, Facer of the Facts, Giver of the Straight Poop:
TO DESPERATE, Greetings: O widow art thou not Greek? Dost thou not know the Greeks? A Greek will call it anything: experimental humanism, Platonic dialogues, brotherly love; yet I say it's sodomy! Thy son is a queer! Get him out of that school! Young minds are not made to be opened up; they are made to be filled with Truth and nailed shut! Yet though the hour is late, O widow, all is not lost. Tell thy son he hath another Father which is in Heaven, and that if he shapeth not up, it's boils-and-withered-legs   time. How long will he last with his homo teachers then?

EPISTLE TO THE
CORINTHIANS

DEAR APPY, You know what you are? You're a goddamn egotist, that's what! I counted the number of times "I" appears in your epistles and it averages five per verse. And that's just the short ones. Know something else? You never quote Jesus. You only quote yourself. Who the hell do you think you are? You never even knew Him! Know what? I think you made up that whole dumb story about the Road to Damascus, so you could switch sides and cut out the *real* apostles! Who says your version is right? You do, that's who! Where does Jesus say obey our parents and keep off wine and beat women and children and scourge the flesh and be utterly miserable? Nowhere, that's where! Know what you are, Paulie baby? You're a BORN persecuter, that's what! First you persecute us for BEING Christians, now you're persecuting us for NOT BEING Christian, ENOUGH!! Why don't you do us all a favor and go ascend up your own asshole?   **—FED-UP, CORINTH**
P.S. I bet you don't have the guts to print this!

PAUL, By Appointment to the King of Heaven, Sole Purveyor of the Truth, Chairman of the Board of Faith, Hope, and Charity, and Chief Operating Apostle: (cc: Timotheus, Vice Apostle, Assistant to the Assistant of God, and Guard of His Body)
TO FED-UP, Knowest thou

something? We often feel sorely grieved when the way becometh hard and we are cast down in our spirit. Yet I mindeth not this sort of filthy abuse, for, lo, it simply giveth me one more opportunity to express my great love for my flock. Yea even for the human garbage therein. In fact I welcome injurious words and the unutterable pain they strike into my heart, just as I welcome being flogged with steel-tipped scourges and shipwrecked without sustenance, and having mine testicles crushed in red-hot vises every time I go forth to preach the Word. What straineth my patience howsoever, is when ignorant little Corinthian creeps wound my dearest Savior by rejecting His One and Only Genuine True Teacher, me. That really getteth up my nose.

But lo, it beeth not my job to wreak vengeance on such creeps. That belongeth to God. My job beeth to love them even unto death. Wherefore, Fed-Up, I urge thee to resist the temptation to write further letters like this. The way of forbearance is hard, I know. For surely thou art not as I am, who can kneel before a gorgeous, naked maiden of seventeen years, who danceth and proffereth me wine and drugs and let it not distract me one jot or tittle from pure holy thoughts of my Lord. Yet haply one day thou shalt be strong as I am, humble as I am. In the meantime, be of good cheer. Timotheus and I will call on you when next we are in Corinth, and bring unto you much comfort.
P.S. Thou seest? I print the stinkers also.

HERE ENDETH THE EPISTLES OF THE APOSTLE.

If you would like a copy of any of these Epistles,
send a stamped, addressed messenger to:
DEAR APPY, Station of the Cross, Appian Way, Rome.

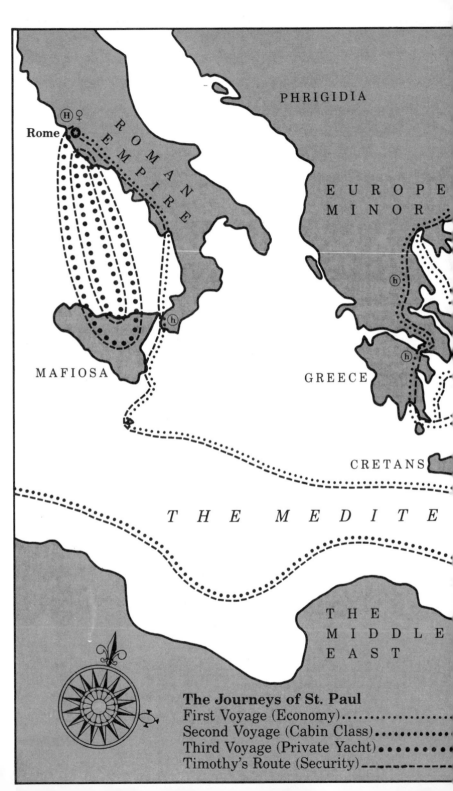

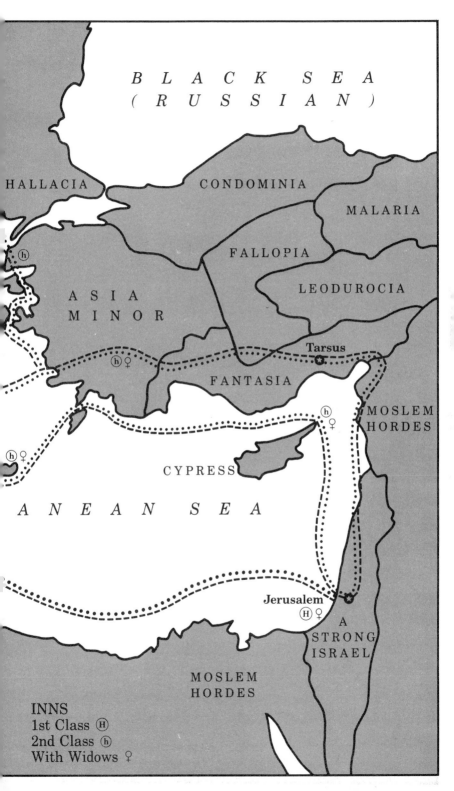

THE AMAZING REVELATION©
OF SAINT ORAL

CHAPTER 1

THE Amazing Revelation of Our Lord and Chief Operating Officer, Jesus Christ, as told *by exclusive arrangement*, to His servant Oral, of those things which must shortly come to pass;

2 Including the terrible Shape of Things to Come, the destruction of His enemies *and those of his servant Oral*, and the Final Show-Down.

3 Blessed be he who readeth this prophecy and heedeth it, and explaineth it to his wife; for the time is at hand.

4 Oral, to his churches and franchises throughout the land, and to ye'all out there who receiveth and believeth;

5 Dearly beloved brethren, ye knowest it beeth a funny thing, but the LORD God seemeth to have singled me out for *special* duty;

6 Yea, Just the other morning, as I sat in mine den, giving testimony unto the LORD and keeping my mind pure and free of *thought*, lo, I heard from behind me a great Voice sounding, like unto a mighty wind:

7 Saying, ORAL, this is the Big Enchilada; what thou art about to see, write it down, and send it unto thy churches and franchises for an modest fee, *postage* not included;

8 And I, Oral, turned to see the Voice from whence it came, and I beheld seven lights each one like unto a color of the *rainbow*.

9 And there smack dab in the midst of them was HIM, and His hair was neat and golden like unto the flake of the corn, and His eyes blazed with love and wrath and His body was girt all about with raiment, even unto the *socks*;

10 And He spake saying, Oral thou art of My Chosen, and thou knowest well that I am He who hath the keys to Heaven and to Heck;

11 And verily I say unto you, that if they hearken not unto the words that I shall inspire you with *exclusively*, yea I shall kill them all dead with death *several times*. But he who hearkeneth to My words and explaineth them unto his wife, to him will I grant a guaranteed *reservation* in Paradise. And to her also.

12 For the LORD God cometh to judge the righteous and the wicked, but mostly the wicked, *real soon*, maybe even in the next couple of weeks.

CHAPTER 2

AFTER this I looked up and, lo, I beheld a screen in the firmament; and I rose and approached and passed through the screen and, would not ye know, I began to *glow*! And I knew that I, little Oral, was privileged to be in Heaven.

2 And I beheld before me, suspended in the void, a triangle, which was a slice as it were, of Pie; and above It shone a great light, which light proceeded from one unblinking Eye. And I knew that the Eye was upon me.

3 And beneath the Eye and the Pie in the sky, I beheld a table of highly polished fruit-wood; and around the table sat four *elders* whose hair was neat and golden like unto wheat which is the breakfast of champions; and they were girt about with white raiment even unto their socks; and before each elder was an golden pad and by each pad an golden pen wherewith each might write;

4 And I heard the voices of many angels about the table; and their number was ten thousands times

a hundred million billion trillion as near as I could tell,

5 Singing with a loud voice, Blessed is the King and Eye,

6 And the elders said, Amen.

7 And behold at the foot of the table was a fifth seat, which was unoccupied; and the elders rose and beckoned unto *me*, smiling, and said, Come forth Oral and take thy place, for thou art one of the Board.

8 And I approached and took my place, whereupon the Eye did wink at me and my heart rejoiced exceedingly.

9 Then saw I a great angel, the which was clean of cut, drawing near to the table of highly polished fruit-wood, proclaiming in a rich bass, Who is *worthy* to open the envelope and loosen the seals thereof?

10 And I, Oral, wept, because no man in heaven or earth was found worthy to open the envelope.

11 But one of the elders, Luke I think it was, said unto me, Weep not Oral, for *thou* hast been chosen to open the envelope and to loose the seals thereof,

12 And he said, May I have the envelope please?

13 Whereupon the angel placed before me a mighty envelope which shone with a great light and on it were seven seals which were of gold and on each seal was written, Pull Here.

14 And I, Oral, loosed the first seal, and heard a noise as of thunder and beheld a white horse; and he who sate thereon had a cockéd hat and he went forth and knockéd everyone into it.

15 And I, Oral, loosed the second seal, and there came forth another horse and on it sate a few good men, the which had helmets and necks that were of leather and power was given unto them to smash and rend and burn and punish and kill in the name of sweet Jesus;

16 And I, Oral, loosed the third seal, and beheld a dark horse, and he that sate thereon had in his hand a pair of galoshes;

17 And I, Oral, was about to loose the fourth seal when one of the Elders spake unto me saying, Hey, Oral, the hour of the LORD is at hand. Getteth thou onto the seventh seal, for that is the *good one.*

18 So I, Oral, loosed the seventh seal.

19 And when the seventh seal had been loosed on the envelope, there was silence in heaven; and verily I thought, it is quiet. Too quiet.

20 But then I beheld the earth of the Coast which did begin to quake; and I beheld eucalyptus trees which were burnt up and green turf which was burnt up and ivy and avocados;

21 And a third part of the people of that place were at the beach, and they were swallowéd up;

22 And another third part were upon the highways and byways and thruways and freeways, in their chariots, and within their chariots was music playing in the rhythms of Satan; and they were swallowéd up;

23 And a third third which were in their houses, touching and clutching each other's nethermost secret portions and smoking white powder, *they too were swallowéd up.*

24 And that made three thirds of the whole shebang.

25 And now there fell from heaven a great star, and smoke issued forth from his mouth and brimstone from his nostrils; and the name of the star was Hollywood, and he fell into the bottomless pit;

26 Then fell the lesser stars and starlets, which were comely in their bodies and whored after riches, stroking one another in public as well as private, which

is an abomination in the eyes of the LORD and maketh him to *puke*!

27 They too fell into the pit and were branded on their haunches like cattle and were gnawed all over by smelly rats and had holes drilled in their private parts and their heads were sliced like bread for ever and ever, Amen.

28 Wherefore the elders and I, Oral, rejoiced and were glad.

CHAPTER 3

AND I saw another sign in heaven, wonderful and marvelous, for across the skies which were red, from corner even unto corner, there appeared a cross of blue, and set therein were stars of white.

2 And from the southeast and from the southwest, yea and even from the deep south came seven angels, risen again, and avenging; and they were pale of hue, and their raiment was all of white, from the peaks of their hoods even unto their socks; and the eyes of them were blue, and the backs of the necks thereof were red;

3 And they were girded about with belts which were like the sun;

4 And each avenging angel bore before him a torch which burned, and its shape was the shape of a cross;

5 And verily, they looked like the Wrath of God.

6 And I heard a voice out of heaven saying, Go your ways, for it is high time this country was turned around.

7 And the first angel went, and with his torch burnt he all the books of their abominations; from off their shelves took he them and made a great pile of those books, whose names were all manner of filth and sedition and mockery and blasphemous words such as "Catch Her in the Rye";

8 And the second angel went, with shears for cutting. And he cut the films of their abominations, yea with a vengeance cut he them, until the spools of film were empty, and the screens whereon they had been showed were empty and likewise were the minds of men.

9 And the third angel went over the fields of grass which were smoking; and he said, Let us spray. And he sprayed the smoking grass with a plague, and the grass died, and likewise the people of the smoking grass;

10 And I heard the angel of the spray saying, Behold, I shall show unto thee who is Most High.

11 And the fourth angel went and unplugged the plugs of the instruments of their abominations, which were noisesome and grievous sore unto the ears of the righteous, and he cast the records thereof, yea and the cassettes also, into the fire.

12 And the fifth angel went into a place where the people were exceeding slothful, and did eat of stamps, which were food, and the people did roll upon the ground in hunger, and repent themselves that they had not been born pale of hue, and righteous.

13 And the sixth angel went into the places of learning and the schools where the truth of the LORD God's creation had been corrupted, and even prayers unto the LORD had been banished and cast out; and with a sharp sword he did inscribe the name of the LORD onto the foreheads and the nethermost quarters of the false prophets who were employed therein.

14 And the seventh angel went unto the Court of Law wherein sate nine judges; and the cloaks thereof were black, though their hearts were red; save two, whose hearts were red and white and blue and faithful unto the Republic of Heaven:

15 And the seven unworthy

judges did he cast down, and the seven avenging angels did succeed them in their places, until the court was packed;

16 And the seven angels and the two judges which were righteous did justify and affirm all that had gone before as right and just and in accordance with the Constitution between God and man;

17 And the great wound which the unrighteous had made, severing the Church from the State and the State from the Church, was *healed* for ever and ever.

CHAPTER 4

THEN there came one of the seven angels which had healed the wound, and spake unto me, personally, Oral, saying unto me, Come hither and I will show unto thee the judgment of the great whore that sitteth upon the eastern sea, and between the rivers:

2 In that city where the Nations which are United against righteousness have builded them a great tower of glass, wherein they do fornicate in the cup of the wine of her abominations;

3 So carried he me away and carried away was I to a city in the north and east, and, lo, I beheld a woman in color like unto an Apple when it is Big; which is red;

4 And the woman was clad in costly raiment which was low-cut revealing the paps which were round and comely, and the skirt of her was slit even unto the thighs, revealing limbs which were tan and lithesome and likewise comely, and as the vision unfolded and she did stretch forth her limbs and her paps, I, Oral, beheld in her navel an golden staple.

5 And beneath her was a name written MISS BABYLON-ON-THE-HUDSON; SCARLET WOMAN OF THE MONTH.

6 And the rulers of the earth did lick up the liquors of her lust; they did suck the secretions of her sexfulness; they did gaze upon her in her comeliness and SPILL THEIR SEED UPON THE GROUND!

7 And I, Oral, was sore afflicted in my brain, and I turned unto the Elders and spake saying, Shall this be allowed in the land of the free?

8 And they smiled a sad little smile and answered, saying, O Oral, it shall get worse before it getteth better, yet fear not, for the righteous shall prevail. Getteth thou not mad, Oral, for we shall get even;

9 Then saw I another great horror in heaven, and this was the worst so far: behold there came a great Red dragon having an hundred and thirty-nine heads and on each head a million horns and on each horn two warts making two hundred and seventy-six million warts in all;

10 And the red dragon had a tail an hundred miles long and upon it there rode a legion of fellows which traveled with it; pointy and pink were their heads and they did sup of wine and water that was imported;

11 And I, Oral, beheld red smoke issuing from the bowels of the dragon;

12 And he made a mess.

13 And the shape of the mess was a star and its color was red.

14 And this was the mark of the dragon, and boy, it was everywhere; yea even on the foreheads of the righteous.

15 And they that rode on the tail of the dragon bound up the righteous in tape so that they might be helpless: and the color of the tape was red.

16 And there was this great canal of water which was the hope of the righteous who had built it and paid for it, which was snatched from them and wrapped

up in gift-wrapping and surrendered to the dragon; and the color of the ribbon was red.

17 And the dragon laughed a laugh that was foreign or I am a Dutchman, and lighted a great cigar and stuck it in his beard; and the tip of this cigar was red.

18 And a great fire did issue from the bowels of the dragon and the T-Bills and CDs, and IRAs and Keogh plans of the righteous were consumed thereby; and the color of the ink and of their ledgers was red.

19 And I, Oral, seeing the triumph of the dragon became wrath and all I could see was red.

20 And I called aloud to the Eye, which had become irritated by all the smoke so that it too was red, and spake saying, LORD shall all the world be red?

21 And the Eye answered me in this wise, Fear not Oral, for the Blood of the Ram shall redeem the free world.

22 And I, Oral, answered, saying, but LORD is not the blood of the Ram red also?

23 And the Eye replied, Uh-uh. The blood of the Ram is red *and* white *and* blue!

24 And I, Oral, said, OK LORD.

25 And the Eye said, Not to worry.

CHAPTER 5

THEN, I, Oral, beheld the greatest wonder to date; Lo, a great Ram appeared, that was white all over and neatly shorn. And his face was the face of a man and clean of cut; and on his head was an set of mighty horns, and his hindquarters were modestly covered.

2 And before the Ram was a mighty bed, of brass, whose feet were of brass and the mattress of which was firm yet not of brass;

3 And on the bed there slept a virgin clothed in white raiment even unto her socks, and she was pure and unsullied and pale of hue;

4 And the Ram stood guard duty over her.

5 And though I, Oral, beheld the might of the horns of the Ram and the muscles rippling beneath his fleece and his firm aggressive stance, yet knew I that he was a Nice Guy:

6 Wherefore I spake unto the Ram saying, Ram, how shall we prevail against the red Dragon?

7 And the Ram answered, Oral, just let me say this. Mighty weapons have I in mine arsenal, which are fuelled with My wrath and tipped with my Mercy. Many times over could they turn mine enemies into the dung of dogs, yet must I give the dragon the chance to turn his stinking paws in the ways of My righteousness.

8 But Ram, I said, Surely thou knoweth that the dragon shall not turn his stinking paws into the ways of thy righteousness?

9 Those are the rules of the game, O Oral, answered the Ram quietly, And I playeth by the rules.

10 Then from forth out of the dragon's bowels there issued a great fat white dove, the which tipped the scales at at least five hundred pounds; and great was the squawking and whining and cooing thereof.

11 And forth from out of the west there flew a plucky little eagle the which was an feather weight at most, and the which was to do battle with the great fat disgusting dove.

12 And great was the battle, for the eagle was too quick for the dove and wounded him a multitude of times until he bled, even from his heart;

13 And the eagle came in for the kill, attacking from the rear; and great was that miscalculation; for as he struck, the dove sate down with an great squawk and crushed the eagle.

14 And though his opponent was down yet the dove stood not back;

15 But grabbed the eagle by the feet and pulled off his wings and tied a knot in his neck.

16 And great was the rejoicing amongst the heads of the dragon; flagons of hell-brew took they and consumed, toasting the dove, and hurling the empties to the ground.

17 And still the Ram moved not, but stood guard duty over the sleeping beauty; yet I, Oral, beheld that his patience was sorely tried.

18 Then the dragon which was fired with liquor and undeterred by the Ram approached the virgin where she lay; and some of its heads did thrust themselves beneath the sheets as they were like to devour the virgin; and others did tell each other stories of foulness in her hearing; and one head did call her up on the phone.

19 Then did great wrath cross the face of the Ram, and his tail did quiver and he spake unto me saying, O Oral, now have I been pushed too far!

20 And I asked saying, Ram what willst thou do?

21 And the Ram answered, Now is come the moment when I must loose my arsenal!

22 And I cried Way to go LORD!

23 And the Ram confirmed, Yet know Oral, that when mine enemies goest, thou goest too, for this is My Final Coming! My vengeance is stiff and it shall burst the world asunder!

24 And I, Oral, said, Wherefore should I care, O LORD, for when thine enemies are put on the fast track to perdition, shall not the righteous in that same instant, be slam-dunked into Paradise?

25 And the Ram answered, Oral thou hast put it in a nutshell!

26 Then took he a black box from beneath his forequarter, and pressed a button therein;

27 Whereupon I beheld the greatest wonder of all; for from all corners of the heavens there issued angels and each angel held a weapon of the Ram;

28 From the north there came a great host of angels, and they formed a cross, and each angel held an AGM-68A air-launched cruise missile capable of delivering an 170-kiloton warhead over a range of twelve hundred miles;

29 And from the east came a great host of angels from beneath the ocean, and they formed a cross, and each held sixteen launching tubes and each tube held a UGM-27C Polaris A-3 with a range of two thousand eight hundred eighty miles and three MIRV 200-kiloton warheads and each warhead had a delivery capability within four hundred feet of its target.

30 And from the west came another great host of great angels which did rise from super-hardened silos, and each of them bore an M-X missile with a range of nine thousand statute miles, and each of them was armed with fifteen or twenty 12A MIRV 335 kiloton warheads not just ten as Congress has been led to believe;

31 And from the south came the hugest angels of all, host upon host thereof, and each of them carried a mighty Titan ICBM LGM-250 GE6 10-megaton warhead with a range of seven thousand two hundred eighty miles, which warheads were the most beloved of the Ram.

32 Then the Ram did target His angels at the dragon; and the dragon which was dallying with the pure white virgin and rubbing his warts on her unsulliedness, was caught unawares;

33 And each angel hurled his weapon at the dragon and struck the dragon within a target range of four hundred feet and destroyed him totally an hundred thousand times;

34 Yet would he not die.

35 For verily I say unto you, our throw-weight was not sufficient.

36 Whereupon the dragon despite our preemptive first strike, was able to cast back his own weapons from every head of his body; and their throw-weight was greater than ours and great was the destruction that was wrought. There were bits of angel everywhere.

37 And the Ram, which was bloodied greatly in the exchange, spake unto me, Oral, gently, saying, Oral, It will have to be the Big One.

38 And He readied Himself and sprang into the air, and joined together His forelegs and got His nose down and His horns forward; and flames issued forth from out His nostrils and His hindquarters, and a great light shone all about Him, which was the light of kingdom come;

39 For verily He was the greatest Weapon of them all.

40 And He struck the dragon and exploded. And the dragon exploded. And all the beasts of the field and birds of the air and fishes in the sea exploded. And the mountains and rivers and streams and dams exploded. And the earth and the firmament and every piece of Real Estate therein, exploded. And the Third World exploded and the Second and the First, the righteous along with the wicked. Yea, even my lovely and faithful wife and mine two sons exploded.

41 Naught was left but one wart of the dragon the which did spin aimlessly in empty space;

42 And, Lo, after 4004 years plus 1980-odd, whatever that may add up to, the LORD God destroyed all that he had created, because He was sick and tired of queers, communists, gun-control nuts, Popes, rapists, One-worlders, quiche-nibbling joggers, Negro-coddling judges, foreigners, cripples yammering about ramps, welfare mothers, eco-maniacs, anti-nukers, OPEC blackmailers, knee-jerk Liberals, Big Labor, godless, bearded abortionists, dope-sucking rock 'n rollers, Keynesian giveaway specialists, and the kind of scum that call other people's wives on the phone;

43 So he killed them all, and they were cast down into hell where they continued to explode for all eternity;

44 And the righteous killed He also so that He might have them for ever and ever with Him, singing and praising Him for all eternity and never having to worry about sex, or listen to bad news on the TV but to be happy for ever, and tucked up every night.

45 And I, Oral, beheld all this.

46 And, lo, it shall be true, and shall come to pass, for the LORD God hath guaranteed it. Nor is one jot or tittle to be added hereto, for it is His truth, and whomsoever shall add to it, shall have rats gnaw his brain for ever and ever.

47 But he who believeth on it, and explaineth it to his wife, and maketh sure she understandeth it, to him shall be granted the heated swimming pool of eternal life.

48 For ever and ever Amen, all rights reserved.

THE END OF THE NEO-TESTAMENT

A

alms, give in secret, Mt 6:1

_____, tax deductible, Rgn 81

B

Babylon, whore of. See Pope

_____, all change at, LIRR

Bartholomew, apostle Mk 3:18; called Nathanael, Jn 1:45

Body, Mystical. See bowels, dung, emerods, issue of blood, loins, reins, secrets, seed, worms

bosom, Abraham's. See dugs, paps, hooters

Broadway, to destruction. see Square, Times

C

cheek, turn other, Mt 5:39, Lk 6:29. See also Deterrent, Credible

Church. See State

D

devils, possession by, Mt 12:22

_____, repossession by, Mt 12:45

_____, dispossession by Pnma 79

E

entertain, some have e. angels, He 13:2

_____, non-deductible, Dole 82

F

faithful, servant wise and, Mt 24:45. See also Nubians

_____, wife. See Mrs. McJorrity (no calls, please!)

figs, passim

foreskin, a big drawback, Rom 2:25

fornication, filthiness of, Rev 17:4

_____, wine of her, Rev 17:2

_____, wine of the wrath of her, Rev 18:3

_____, obsessed by, Rev passim

G

gay clothing, Jas 2:3. See also Drag

Ghost, Holy, sin against. See Medicare

_____, story. See Lazarus

_____, writers. See Mt, Mk, Lk, Jn

Grace, Amazing. See Burns and Allen

_____, before meals, Lk 22:15

_____, under pressure, Hem 47

H

holy, unto dogs, Mt 7:6

_____ cow. See Rizzuto, Phil

_____ Ghost, body a Temple of. See Hand, cut off, Eye, plucked out, Eunuchs, self-made

J

James, the Greater, Mk 1:19

_____, the Lesser, Lk 6:15

_____, the Mediocre, Jas 1-5

Jehosophat, Jumping. See Moses, Holy

John, the Baptist, Lk 3:1-8

_____, the Southern Baptist, Cnnly 63

K

Kingdom, not of this world, Jn 18:26. See also Church, State

L

Lord, praise. See Ammunition, pass

lump, be ye a, I Co 5:7

A CONCORDANCE TO THE NEO-TESTAMENT

M

Mary, marries Joseph, Mt 1:24

———, mother of Jesus, Lk 2:17

———, mother of many other children, Mt 12:46, Mk 3:13, Lk 8:19

———, Ever virgin, passim

money, disciples to carry none, Lk 9:3

———, evangelists' great need for, passim

mystery, of the Kingdom, Mt 13:11

——— of the Old Mill, Hdy Bys 37

N

need, unto each according to his, Acts 4:34. See also Communism

O

orders, Holy, just following. See Paul, passim

P

Peter. See Rock

Peter, Paul, and Mary. See Folk Rock

Pope. See Antichrist

pray, in secret, Mt 6:6

———, in classrooms, Hlms 82

publicans: tax collectors; antonym, Republicans

R

rebellion. See Romanism, Rum

Road to Damascus. See Hope. See also Crosby, Lamour

Romanism. See Rum, Rebellion

Rum. See Rebellion, Romanism

S

Salmon, ancestor of Jesus, Lk 19:17

———, Janet Evening, Hmstn 1950

seed, mustard. See Salt of Earth, Spice of Life

———, scattered, Mt 13:4

———, spilled, passim

Simon Magus, evil man who offered money for power of Holy Spirit, stopped payment on pledge check, died, went to hell

socks, shepherds wash by night, Lk 2:8

stoned, St. Stephen. See Grass, flesh is as

T

treasure, where t. is, there is heart, Mt 6:21. See also Knox, John, Knox, Fort

trees, walking, Mk 8:24

V

vipers, generation of. See Kids today

virgin, authorized, Mt 1:23

W

wine, -bibber, Jesus called a, Mt 11:19

———, Jesus turns water into, Jn 2

———, old better than new, Lk 5:39

———, Paul advises Tim. to drink, I Tim 5:23

———, promised in Paradise, Mk 14:23

———, utterly forbidden, Vlstd 1917

womb, fruit of. See Loom. See also At the Inn, no

Z

Zebedee, short for Zebedee-doo-dah. See South, Song of the

Oral McJorrity has been called, among other things, a "charismatic and controversial crusader for Christ." He is known and loved by millions, through his daily television appearances on The Six Ninety Five Club (check local listings for time and channel), and by his lovely and faithful wife and sons.

Born and raised in Comstock, West Virginia, he became an ordained minister at age 15, after a typical American boyhood. He is the recipient of an honorary Doctor of Divinity degree from Oral State© University, and has walked with, talked with, and put the fear of the Lord into elected officials all over this great land.

From such humble beginnings, with God's help, he has risen to a position of great influence in the media, government, medicine, science, education, adolescent dating etiquette, and national defense.

Tony Hendra was born in London at the height of the blitz. This gave him a profound insight into the transience of earthly things, and a squint. The nuns got him before he was seven, and now, though he no longer knows what eternity means, they have him for all eternity. A brief teenage sojourn as a Benedictine novice led inevitably to a career in humor, which has left him considerably poorer than if he'd taken a vow of poverty. He lives in Sodom on the Hudson, worships his two daughters, kicks his dog, and has insomnia in the nude.

Sean Kelly is an excommunicated Catholic, an expatriot Canadian, an expelled English teacher, and the ex-editor of *National Lampoon* and *Heavy Metal* magazines. He has also written a great deal of what passes for comedy on television. Much to his own surprise, and the surprise of all who know him, he has a beautiful wife and four baptized children.